*Straight A's Never Made
Anybody Rich*

STRAIGHT A'S NEVER MADE ANYBODY RICH

Wess Roberts, Ph.D.

author, *Leadership Secrets of Attila the Hun*

HarperCollins*Publishers*

HarperCollins*Publishers*
77–85 Fulham Palace Road,
Hammersmith, London W6 8JB

Published by HarperCollins*Publishers* 1991
1 3 5 7 9 8 6 4 2

Copyright © Wess Roberts 1991

The Author asserts the moral right to
be identified as the author of this work

A catalogue record for this book
is available from the British Library

ISBN 0 246 13886 6

Set in Century Old Style

Printed in Great Britain by
HarperCollinsManufacturing Glasgow

*This book is for Cheryl, Justin, Jaime,
and Jeremy, who understand the difference
between grades and an education, and
the distinction between having material
wealth and living well.*

Contents

Contents

Acknowledgments

While this work is my own and I accept full responsibility for any faults or flaws it may contain, it is appropriate to acknowledge the assistance of those people who have helped me. To that end, I am particularly indebted to Richard Pine who helped me develop the idea for the book and who placed it with HarperCollins. Arthur Pine and Lori Andiman, who are also members of the Arthur Pine Associates team, were also genuinely supportive and helpful during the entire writing process.

Dr. Hendrie Weisinger offered me a number of first-rate ideas and perceptions on personal achievement, and I thank him for his continuing support of my writing efforts. My mentor and good friend Lee Allen provided me with a wealth of insight pertinent to personal achievement for young people as well as for adults.

Thanks, Lee. I owe special acknowledgment and thanks to my friend Hugh Dougherty, a retired banking executive who also had a successful second career in construction, for his assistance in reviewing each chapter as it was completed. During the last five years I have learned many important concepts of career and personal success from him. Many of his ideas are incorporated in this book. Ellen Roddick deserves heartfelt thanks for helping me clarify some important points and clean up the syntax in the manuscript, and special thanks to Theresa Clarey and Amanda Bostian for helping me with the final stages of putting the manuscript together.

I am especially grateful to Eddie Bell and Ed Breslin at HarperCollins for their direction and guidance in all phases of this book. Both of them are truly outstanding publishing professionals, a pleasure to work with, and have added considerable value to the overall project. I am also appreciative of the personal interest and support shown by George Craig, who is by any standard one of the great corporate leaders today. To Geoff Hannell and Sandi Borger and all of the other people at HarperCollins who have helped in any way with the book's production, marketing, and distribution, I express my sincere appreciation for a job well done.

As always I have been fortunate to have Cheryl and our children—Justin, Jaime, and Jeremy—extend their patience and understanding to me during the time in which I wrote this book. Cheryl was always available to give me ideas and insights that helped me focus on the essences of the points being made and to provide me with reassurance when needed. Justin provided me with creative input and helped with the book's continuity. Jaime and Jeremy read drafts of the manuscript and gave me clever suggestions for its improvement.

And finally, I am grateful to all of the really successful people who unselfishly share their time and talents with others, for they help make the world a better place for all to enjoy.

Introduction

This book is about breaking through false barriers that keep people from realizing their full potential. Its central thesis is that the satisfaction of personal achievement is accompanied by self-confidence and a sense of personal worth when you do your best at whatever you do. This feeling of wholeness and success is never achieved easily—but it is one of life's great joys.

Straight A's Never Made Anybody Rich contrasts boldly with books on personal achievement that contain false promises of fame and fortune; as a matter of fact, it accepts neither as a sign of success. Rather, here is a book about how we all can achieve happiness in our personal lives and be successful in our careers—regardless of our social status or how much money we make.

To dispel any notion that the book's title implies

that good grades are totally irrelevant to accomplishment, I want to make it clear that I believe in rewarding students with A's for meeting high academic standards. Moreover, I'm an avid supporter of lifelong education and personal growth. At the same time, I believe that people should have the right to earn as much money as they want to—as long as they earn it honestly.

But academic achievement and wealth do not necessarily go hand in hand. And they certainly don't guarantee either satisfaction or happiness. Nor do they entitle anyone to feel superior. They are not even necessary for achievement: Many accomplished people never excelled academically or amassed personal fortunes.

Beginning at birth, you are compared to other children. Early criteria for comparison include your birth weight and height, your age when you first begin to crawl and then to walk, and your age when you utter your first word. On it goes throughout your entire life.

Although we are not born with equal talents, abilities, and opportunities, we are frequently compared to each other and placed on a spectrum of achievement that runs from excellent to inadequate. Once so placed, we may feel confined and limited.

Nowhere is the obsession with measuring personal ability and achievement more obvious than in the typical scholastic grading system. Students are commonly compared to their classmates by being assigned grades based on a grading curve. Yet those grades are so unreliable that standardized achievement tests are used as a second measure of academic ability. Although both grades and achievement test scores have certain utility, they ignore many significant factors. They do not, for instance, measure quality of educational experience, ability to think critically, intuition, interest in academic subjects, ability to get along with other people, creativity, or entrepreneurial potential. These and other ingredients essential to personal achievement beyond the classroom door are too often overlooked in the process of education.

Measuring individual differences produces both desirable and undesirable results. On the positive side is development of a competitive spirit that can propel us to high levels of personal performance. A negative consequence is the construction of false barriers that can hold back capable and substantial people.

When we compare ourselves unfavorably with other people in terms of academic performance and wealth, we may undermine our own self-confidence and become too discouraged to strive effectively to fulfill our own potential—which is what personal achievement is all about.

Personal achievement requires drive and determination, intelligence and ingenuity. In many ways, our lives today are more complex than lives lived in simpler, more predictable times. But common convictions unite those who make the most of their talents and abilities at any age.

This book explores the convictions, behavior, skills, abilities, and values that are characteristic of high achievers. It is based on my work as a professional in corporate human resource development.

Throughout the book, I provide case studies that

illustrate the triumph of personal achievement. They are drawn from the lives of people I have worked with over the years. You will read about their strengths, weaknesses, mistakes, and accomplishments. Collectively, I believe their stories illustrate the search and the struggle to meet major challenges that most of us confront. With the exception of Pete Bucher, these case studies obscure the true identities of the people involved. So I don't use real names or portray actual families. To do so would only upset those who might feel they should have been included and anger those who might feel that their privacy has been invaded.

You will notice my irreverence toward the attitude of "entitlement." For this I make no apology. Truly successful people do not limit themselves to entitled achievement. They feel obligated to make the world a better place for everyone and don't think of themselves as having an automatic exclusive right to success. Those who see entitlement as the key ingredient to achieving success are most comfortable draining other people of their finest qualities.

The definition of success can be argued. In the end, however, the only thing that matters is how we measure up to our own talents and abilities. No one has the right to expect more from us than we have to offer. Yet too many of us worry more about what other people want from us than about what we are able to give. Living is a process of maturing and developing. Success does not arrive at a single magic moment. Strangely enough disappointments frequently occur when we are closest to our most solid achievements.

It is my aim to engage your curiosity and interest

while providing you with useful strategies for making the most of your talents and abilities. To this end, I hope the book's message encourages not only those who, in the words of Henry David Thoreau, "live lives of quiet desperation," but also those who simply need to clarify their values and priorities.

*Straight A's Never Made
Anybody Rich*

1

Skool Daze

Once upon a time, a teacher and her first-grade students spent a school year together in a little red schoolhouse. The teacher wanted her students to learn all of the material prescribed for the year. And so it was that she had spent the summer vacation reviewing new curriculum materials, writing lesson plans, preparing student handouts, developing tests, outlining homework assignments, and planning field trips.

Her students had spent the summer with their families doing the kinds of things that five and six year olds did in their town.

On the first day of school, the students and teacher met in their classroom. "Who would like to learn how to read better?" the teacher asked her class, for these were students who were just learning to read.

"Can we learn to read sports magazines?" asked Kevin, who liked to watch and talk about professional baseball and basketball.

"I don't like reading. Can't you just read us a story?" asked Robert.

"Can we read stories about animals?" asked Megan, who liked to visit the zoo.

"Why can't we just have a longer recess instead?" asked Rod, who showed no initial interest in reading.

"I'm hungry!" said Amanda, who was always munching on something.

"My stomach hurts. Can I go see the nurse?" asked Bruce, who seemed to be ill.

"I like to read," said Louise, who appeared to be the class brain.

And the teacher taught her class to read at the first-grade level.

On the second day of school, the class and the teacher met again in their classroom. "Who would like me to teach arithmetic today?" she inquired.

"I don't need to learn how to count," said Kevin. "I'm going to have a computer when I get big."

"Counting doesn't seem like much fun," said Robert.

"I'll never be very good in arithmetic!" Megan exclaimed.

"I don't want to learn how to add and subtract things," stated Rod. "Let's play kickball instead."

"How long before lunch?" Amanda inquired.

"Arithmetic gives me a headache," said Bruce.

"I like arithmetic!" shouted Louise. "Can we learn how to use computers too?"

And the teacher taught arithmetic to her class.

On the third day of school, the class and the teacher met in their classroom. "Who would like to learn how to write?" she asked her class.

"I want to learn how to sign autographs," said Kevin. "I'm going to be a basketball player when I grow up."

"Can we have music time? Writing doesn't sound like fun," said Robert.

"Yeah!" shouted Megan. "I'll write notes to everyone in the class. Can I get extra credit if I write the principal a letter?"

"Why do we need to learn how to write?" asked Rod. "We're only in the first grade."

"Can we write a note to the cooks in the cafeteria, and tell them what we want for lunch?" asked Amanda.

"Writing makes my hand hurt," said Bruce.

"I'd like to learn how to write," said Louise.

And the teacher taught the children how to write.

On the fourth day of school, the teacher assembled her students in their classroom.

"Who has their homework ready to hand in?" the teacher asked.

"I was playing with my friends last night. Is it okay if I turn it in tomorrow?" asked Kevin.

"I couldn't find my homework assignment sheet," said Robert.

"I didn't have time to do my homework. I was talk-

3

ing to my friends until I went to bed last night," reported Megan.

"I don't like homework," said Rod.

"I think I left my homework in the cafeteria yesterday," said Amanda.

"Homework makes me want to throw up," mumbled Bruce.

"Thanks for sharing that with us, Bruce," someone said as the class groaned in unison.

"Here's my homework; I hope it is what you wanted," said Louise.

And the teacher graded the class on their homework assignments, giving F's to all the children who failed to hand in their work.

On the fifth day of school, the students met the teacher in their classroom. "Who is ready for the test?" asked the teacher.

"I don't want to take a test, but thanks just the same," said Kevin.

"Test? What test?" asked Robert, who hadn't paid attention earlier in the week.

"Do the boys have to take it too?" Megan asked.

"I'm not very good at tests," Rod said.

"Can we go to lunch first?" asked Amanda.

"Can I go to the bathroom?" asked Bruce.

"I studied last night. I'm ready," said Louise.

And so the teacher gave her students their test.

After a while, the teacher sent home a note with each student inviting the parents to parent-teacher conferences. "Whose parents will be coming to the parent-teacher conferences?" asked the teacher.

"My dad is coaching his baseball team tonight, and my mom is working in the snack bar," reported Kevin.

"My parents are taking me to a concert tonight," said Robert.

"I left the note at one of my friend's houses," said Megan. "My parents don't know about it."

"My parents don't like parent-teacher conferences," said Rod.

"We're going out to dinner tonight. Mom and Dad want to know if they can come another time," said Amanda.

"My mom and dad said to tell you that they're not feeling well," said Bruce.

"My parents will be here," said Louise.

And the teacher held a parent-teacher conference with Louise's parents.

A few years later, the teacher went to visit her former students who were now in the twelfth grade. "How's everyone doing?" the teacher asked.

"I hurt my knee playing soccer last summer. The doctor says I can't play sports anymore," said Kevin.

"I'm in a band," said Robert.

Megan wasn't present. She was married and had a year-old baby.

No one knew where Rod was. He just stopped coming to school one day.

"I've been on a diet," said Amanda.

"I like school now," said Bruce.

"I'm going to college next year," said Louise.

And the teacher looked forward to her next visit with her former students.

A few years passed, and they met again. "How's everyone doing?" the teacher asked.

"I own a sporting goods store," said Kevin.

"My band is doing well," said Robert.

"I'm doing much better," said Megan. "I took the GED (General Education Development) exams, and now I'm enrolled in college. Although it is, at times, a little frustrating taking care of the family and studying too."

"I couldn't find any work I liked, so I'm going to a vocational school where I'm learning how to be an electrician," said Rod, who had returned for the class reunion.

"I'm a dietitian," said Amanda.

"I'm a doctor," said Bruce. "Now whenever I get sick, I just prescribe myself some medicine."

"I'm a schoolteacher," said Louise.

And the story began anew.

Arriving by bus, car, van, bicycle, skateboard, subway, or foot, millions of youngsters descend on public and private classrooms as each new school year begins.

The effects of heredity and environment make each child different. Yet children are similar in many ways too. Their differences endow them with individuality; their similarities bind them by common needs.

Some are born into middle-class families while others live in abject poverty. A few begin life amid an abundance of material possessions. Some have many siblings. Others are only children. Some live in foster homes; some have been adopted at birth or in early childhood. Most live with one or both of their birth parents. More and more of them have been emotionally affected by a parent's death or by divorce. In the United States, a growing number belong to ethnic or racial minorities.

Today when many of the frightening diseases that once plagued humankind have been eradicated, some children are burdened with heartbreaking birth defects, congenital diseases, or predispositions to medical and psychological maladies.

Some children are tall, others short; most, of course, are about average in height. A few are grossly overweight; others are frighteningly thin. Average-looking children resemble the ones pictured on breakfast cereal boxes. A few have striking physical beauty, and others are seen as unattractive.

Attempts at friendship are occasionally frustrated by petty jealousies, fights in the hallways, bouts of name-calling, and fleeting moments of utter hatred for one another.

In elementary school, children form a few lasting friendships. The constant pressures of scholastic, athletic, social and extracurricular competition notwithstanding, they socialize and cooperate with one another fairly well. At the same time, they seek peer acceptance to gain a sense of personal worth. They vacillate between riding a wave of happiness and wallowing in a trough of despair.

During their teenage years, they become restless and struggle for personal and collective independence from the control of adults. Some practice restraint in this effort and others rebel forcefully. A few become hopelessly lost, destined to live outside generally accepted societal norms.

Students are shown educational films and given lectures about the use of substances unhealthy for human consumption. And for the most part, they believe these messages—although not all heed them. The fortunate ones who adopt constructive ways to cope with life's difficulties gain a personal advantage. Few if any, however, will be totally untouched by decadence, widespread crime, corruption, greed, rampant use of both illicit and legal drugs, and the moral decay that color the sunset years of the twentieth century.

Their attitudes toward education range from anxious engagement to blatant stoicism. The majority of them attend school because it is what society expects of them and because they enjoy it. There are, of course, those who consider going to school no more a voluntary activity than serving a twelve-year prison sentence with time off during the summer months.

The distribution of academic talent extends from the gifted to the dim. The majority of students are scattered along a spectrum between these two extremes. Many teachers, for whatever reason, focus on average students—shortchanging both the gifted and the slow learners.

Students across the land are exposed to a uniform core curriculum in public and private schools. Beyond this core, there are vast differences in curricula and the quality of the faculties and facilities. Often the facilities receive too much attention.

Learning can take place in a humble setting if the teachers and the curriculum are good and the students want to learn.

It may come as a shock to well-meaning administrators who fight hard to improve faculty salaries and to build better facilities—but a fine education isn't made of brick and mortar, labs and gymnasiums, or cafeterias and playgrounds. It isn't measured by standardized achievement tests that pigeonhole students and evaluate schools. And the best teachers aren't necessarily the best-paid teachers. Rather, education is a messy, often disorderly and sometimes flawed process guided by dedicated teachers. They work with parents to enable children to learn as much as they can. Teachers and parents can also help students develop healthy patterns of behavior and self-esteem, while preparing them to discover as adults that learning never ends and you need not outgrow your ability to progress.

Reflections on Skool Daze

During your school days, you experience structured learning and chaotic emotions. In retrospect, you may feel as if you spent these years in a daze, as memories become misty. Yet your school experiences are formative in such areas as self-esteem, integrity, perseverance, tenacity, and self-confidence. As a child, you don't suspect the long-term impact your school days will have on you. Little do you realize that early experiences predispose you to make the choices you make later in life.

As a small child, you don't have the ability to make informed judgments. Your behavior is largely instinctive. In this phase of life, you rely on primary adult caretakers (usually parents), teachers, and counselors, not only to care for and nurture you, but also to guide you and make decisions for you. Your early values are based on those to which you are exposed. As you mature, you attend to your own basic survival needs. You begin to make choices. Influenced by your broadening experiences, you either conform to the values of your youth or adopt new ones to govern your adult life.

Modern societies have established high-school graduation as a common goal for young people. In primary and secondary school, many events and activities nurture, shape, and develop you. To some extent, during your school days you dream about what the future holds. Your parents offer advice about what they believe to be within your grasp. Your teachers not only educate you but also prepare you to compete for the best positions—whatever your chosen career. At this juncture, however, neither they nor you fully comprehend the boundaries of your real potential or the direction in which your long-term interests may take you.

All students are exposed to bias of one sort or another and have some trials and tribulations along the way. In the beginning, students with supportive families have more advantages than the rest. Over time, these advantages may be leveraged into increasingly advantageous skills and abilities. There are also students who fail to develop their natural abilities fully—and eventually lose them. And some students never learn to cope during school days. Too many young people develop habits that, without meaningful intervention, will eventually lead them to a lifetime of lasting frustration and despair.

Lessons Learned from Skool Daze

The adversities you face as a young child resemble adversities that you confront as an adult. Although many of these provide valuable lessons, you don't recognize them at first. As you mature, you begin to cope effectively with and to work through tough challenges.

And so it is that everyone's Skool Daze provide valuable lessons that dispense hope, strength, and courage all the days of your life. These are a few of the lessons to be learned from your Skool Daze:

• There are many paths to personal achievement. Often education and training lead you to the opportunity to make the most of your life.

• A teacher's job is to teach—to help you gain skills and knowledge. As a student, it is your responsibility to learn—even though it is sometimes convenient to blame poor teachers when you don't.

• Whether you have earned straight A's or lesser grades, whether you are endowed with material riches or get by with something less, you are the master of your own destiny.

• After you've done all you can to learn a new skill or to broaden your knowledge, you've earned the right to be proud of your efforts regardless of the grade you receive. (Remembering this point will help you become consistent and dependable, instilling in you a sense of self-worth, and all of these qualities are far more important than sheer brilliance.)

• However poorly you perform in school, only you (not your grades) can keep you from learning in the future the things you need to know to have a meaningful and productive life. Nonetheless, learn as much as you can while you're in school!

• Arriving at a major milestone is always more rewarding if you had fun while your were getting there. So enjoy each year of your schooling—and you will enjoy graduation day all the more.

• Your school days illustrate how personal achievement is sometimes arrived at by a journey down a serpentine trail. Progress toward your goals often requires you to take steps sideways and even backward. But to graduate—or to accomplish other goals—you need to remember to take more steps forward than in any other direction.

• As a student, to arrive at the place you've set out to reach—promotion to the next grade and eventually graduation—you will have to endure difficulties and face challenges. From time to time, therefore, correct the course you've set.

• And last, remember the ultimate goal of your school days is not only to learn what you don't know but also to learn how to find out what you still need to know. Education is a lifelong process.

2

The Quest for Success

Charles Dickens, the preeminent English novelist, had a difficult childhood. His father was perpetually in debt and as a consequence was sent to debtors' prison, a common punishment at the time. Denied an education by his parents' misfortune Dickens went to work in a blacking factory at the age of twelve; later he moved on to other jobs, developing a lifelong habit of working hard. His novels include *Oliver Twist, A Tale of Two Cities, Great Expectations, Hard Times, Our Mutual Friend, Little Dorrit,* and *David Copperfield.* In each of his novels, Dickens found a way to proclaim his own faith in the supremacy of good and its eventual triumph over evil.

Wilkins Micawber, a lawyer, is one of the principal characters in Dickens's admittedly autobiographical novel *David Copperfield.* Mr. Micawber's comic character is a man with a flare for writing flamboyant letters and giving soapy speeches. Constantly besieged by unpaid creditors, Micawber (like Dickens's own father) experiences a stay in debtors' prison where he is joined by his family—an option extended to families at that time.

Ever the optimist, Micawber reappears throughout the novel. Micawber always seems to be there when his friend David Copperfield needs him. There is hardly any fault to be found in hoping to have friends who can be counted on in your own troubled times, although many of your assumed friends may actually desert you when you are down.

Blessed with faith in better fortune to come, Micawber is tried and tested, yet sanguinely endures. As the novel ends, Micawber seeks a new start in life by sailing with his family to Australia. There, as David Copperfield learns, Mr. Micawber becomes a successful magistrate. Once again, Dickens depicts good as eventually triumphing.

Jeff and Miriam were classmates. Their teachers and friends thought highly of them, although they were not dedicated students. They both took their school days in stride and appeared to be happy. They always did their best whenever they were interested in what they were doing, both in and out of the classroom. Their teachers encouraged their sporadic efforts at schoolwork, urging them to do better by applying themselves to the subjects that bored them as well as the ones that did not. Both had parents that helped them develop healthy self-esteem and a positive sense of personal worth. Both were popular.

Although he never behaved as if he felt superior, Jeff came from an influential and affluent family. Miriam's family had fewer advantages but her parents taught her that being poor has nothing to do with money—it is a state of mind—and consequently Miriam never behaved as if she were poor.

Jeff and Miriam didn't cause any serious trouble at school, but it wasn't uncommon for either of them to be called into the principal's office for counseling about their pranks or their lack of effort academically.

Most of their homework assignments were handed in on time. If Miriam or Jeff thought a subject was useful, they studied for exams. Otherwise, both gave fleeting glances at their own notes, or at another student's, and attacked the test with abandon—hoping the odds on guessing the right answers would be with them. Quite frankly, the fact that some classes bored them was clear in the marks they earned.

If the biology lab assignment for the day was to dissect a frog, Jeff eagerly participated. If it was to dissect a worm, Miriam would do that, and, for a few bucks, she would swallow one of the leftovers just to prove that she could meet the challenge.

Both were active in sports. Miriam was the star of the girls' marching team and often choreographed their high-stepping routines. Of course, her high-school marching team was no match for the professional Dallas Cowboy Cheerleaders, but the other students liked their spirited performances during halftime at football and basketball games.

For two years, Jeff was a substitute interior offensive lineman on the junior-varsity football team. As a senior, he gained a place on the varsity squad but didn't have any playing time until one of the first-team players sustained a season-ending injury. Even then, the only time Jeff got any real notice was when he forgot to run out on the field when his team controlled the ball and he was supposed to be there. But this lackluster career wasn't Jeff's fault; it is simply the destiny of most interior offensive linemen on high-school football teams not to gain much respect or distinction. Luckily, Jeff wasn't playing for fame or for a college athletic scholarship. He played because he wanted to be one of the boys, and most of his friends were on the football team.

Both Miriam and Jeff were in the supporting casts of several high-school plays. Neither of them expected a leading role, and both would have been just as happy handing out programs at the door or working backstage.

Everyone was impressed that a rich kid like Jeff spent many weeks in the summer hauling hay for local farmers. Between hay cuttings, Jeff joined up with Paul and his other rich-kid buddies at a private summer camp. Having learned to tie fancy flies for trout fishing, Jeff often ventured to remote mountain streams where he proudly tested his handiwork. Frequently returning empty-handed, Jeff wasn't too proud to gobble up a kettle full of the trout Paul had landed from the camp's prestocked pond.

Miriam spent her summers tending her younger brother and sister while their parents worked. She and her older brother were partners in a front-porch business—they sold worms to early-morning fishermen. It helped her earn money to buy new clothes for the next school year. Clothes were important to Miriam and Jeff, but not too important. Both wore clothes that made them feel comfortable. Nothing else mattered much—they had their own standards if not style.

After twelve years in elementary and secondary school, they arrived at a major turning point—high-school graduation. As they moved on to higher education, Jeff and Miriam took different paths toward success. Important decisions were made—ones that would affect their adult lives. They now took very divergent paths. Jeff was accepted by an Ivy League college. Miriam enrolled at a local junior college and planned to complete her bachelor of arts degree in English at a state college.

Reflections on
the Quest for Success

In Dickens's *David Copperfield*, the comic character Micawber strived to overcome many obstacles and finally discovered a place where he could find the success that had eluded him. He was a man of whimsical dreams, even fantasy. Interned in the debtors' prison of the day, Micawber was joined there by his family. They never gave up on him, and he never gave up his quest for success.

Along the way both Jeff and Miriam made some mistakes and missed a few opportunities to do exciting things. In school they were very much alike. But their families and the colleges they attended were very different. Their similarities would not entitle them to, nor would their differences prohibit them from, achieving success. Whatever they accomplished in high school was the foundation on which each would build. As they graduated from high school, Jeff and Miriam were fortunate to have enjoyed their school days and to be remembered well by their teachers and classmates. Most important, Jeff and Miriam entered their young adult lives without looking back at the past in anguish, and neither feared the future.

Lessons Learned from the Quest for Success

There is something to be learned by studying the comical Micawber and the ordinary Jeff and Miriam. Micawber illustrates Dickens's belief that if one doesn't give up and does have faith in better things, good will eventually prevail. Although this idea is inspiring it doesn't always prove true. Yet you, like Micawber, can find a place (and it doesn't have to be Australia) where you can succeed.

Jeff and Miriam are real people—authors of their own personal achievements. They are the ones who will pen their own autobiographies at some future date, regardless of whether or not their individual stories are written for others to read. They have enjoyed their lives so far. They have made choices that seemed right for them and will make even more important choices when they decide how they will spend their adult lives. Both will make mistakes. Some of these will be painful errors because neither Jeff nor Miriam has a script to his or her own destiny.

And so it is with you. There are no entitlements to personal achievement. You have to make choices as you chart your own destiny each day. Here, then, are some thoughts that may serve you along the way:

• In the daily lives of real people, success is most likely to come to him or her who never gives up but rather works toward personal success.

• As an adult, you are a creature of the habits you developed in your youth. And it is easier to develop good habits when you're young than to change bad habits when you're older.

• Success doesn't magically arrive as a prize inside a breakfast cereal box. If you want to make something of yourself, no matter what hand you have been dealt, you must have faith in your ability to play your hand in a practical, realistic, and sometimes risky way.

• The quest for success never ends. It must be continued every day. Once a goal has been achieved, it is replaced with another goal.

• Putting your best effort into completing homework assignments forms habits that distinguish you from those who don't. In school and all aspects of your life, results come from work. No work, no results.

• Competition for grades is like any other competition. The harder you try, the better you are prepared to win.

• While learning something new, never be afraid to ask for help. No one is expected to learn everything by himself or herself. The only shame is in not asking for help when you suspect you need it.

• Students who study together may learn more than those who study alone. People who work together may achieve more than members of the same group working independently. So teamwork is important.

• Classmates in school are like peers at work—you won't like them all, and on some level, you'll compete against them for rewards and recognition. But you'll be expected to get along with them.

• Teachers who only teach you answers to tests, cheat you out of an education.

• Neither school nor the workplace is always interesting and fun, but you're expected to show up and do your best.

• Extracurricular activities during your school days are like hobbies and other outside interests when you become a working adult. You don't have to participate in extracurricular activities to be a good student or have hobbies or outside interests to be good at your job. But without them, your self-concept is hostage to school or job. As a result, your life will probably become uninteresting to you and to other people as well.

• If you think getting an education is an arduous task, consider the consequences of not having the proper education or training when you apply for a job you really want.

• Having an education doesn't guarantee success, but not having one surely diminishes your opportunities.

• Your education won't end when your school days are over unless you are intent on becoming obsolete.

• As a final thought on the quest for success, if you've passed up the opportunity to gain an education, you can't turn back time to improve that decision. But you can begin today to prepare yourself for the job or career you want to have tomorrow.

3

*If It Weren't for Caterpillars,
There Wouldn't Be Any Butterflies*

Metamorphosis is the passage from one state or condition to another. In nature there are many levels of metamorphoses. The changes that occur during metamorphosis range from dramatic to slight. During their life cycle, butterflies undergo complicated changes, while silverfish sustain only minimal alterations.

The four-stage metamorphosis of a butterfly is amazing. All butterflies begin life as an egg laid singly on the surface of a leaf or stem. Next they become larvae, more commonly referred to as caterpillars. In this second phase of their metamorphosis the caterpillars are ravenous eaters of vegetation. Many of them have hairy bodies and look quite ferocious, so some people are afraid to pick them up. Some can give off an odor when agitated. A few have hairs that can sting or irritate human skin. Most caterpillars, however, are quite harmless to handle. Because they eat foliage, bore into fruit, and are serious pests of cultivated plants, caterpillars aren't usually welcome in backyards.

Moving to the next stage, the caterpillars abruptly stop eating and molt. With its head hanging down, each caterpillar attaches itself by its stomach to a leaf or twig. During this third phase, most butterfly caterpillars spin a tuberculate or sculptured pupal case (the chrysalis) about themselves. Unlike the hardened protective case (the cocoon) of a moth in this stage of development, the chrysalis is soft and the butterfly (chrysalid) hangs unprotected in it.

In the fourth and final stage of the metamorphosis, each butterfly gradually frees itself from its chrysalis. As adults, butterflies are sun-loving insects who usually live only a few weeks. Because they eat by sucking nectar from flowers through a long hollow tongue, called a proboscis, butterflies are valuable pollinators.

The biological process of metamorphosis also happens to human beings. The changes we experience involve physical growth and deterioration, intellectual development, and emotional maturation over the entire course of our lives. We may also experience spiritual transformation.

A wonderful illustration of how people change for the better is found in Frances Hodgson Burnett's novel *The Secret Garden*. The central character is Mary Lennox, a neglected orphan sent to live with her uncle at his huge estate, Misselthwaite Manor.

Mary arrives at her uncle's home as an ill-tempered, plain-looking, spoiled brat. Her uncle is a cripple with a crooked back. Mary spends a lot of time with the maid, Martha, and her brother Dickon. After a short time, Mary also discovers Colin, her uncle's son. The young boy is sickly and, like his father, has a crooked back.

Mary, with the help of a robin, discovers the key to a gate that leads through a wall into a secret garden. Once beautiful and well manicured, it has been left unattended; its gate has been locked tight for the ten years since her aunt died after an accident in the garden.

Mary tells Dickon about the secret garden. She suspects that Dickon used his almost supernatural powers with wild creatures to direct the robin to help her find the key. Mary also tells Colin about the garden, and all three children cultivate it, returning it back to its former beauty. Mary helps Colin overcome his perceived disability—he really isn't a hunchback after all. Out of fear, his father always treated Colin as if he were deformed. Near the end of the story, the master is first shocked and then overjoyed to learn that Colin can walk, that he is normal and healthy, and that under Mary's leadership the children have restored the secret garden to its former radiance. By the end of the book, Mary has become a lovely, sweet, and sensitive young girl.

• • •

Every community has its share of unsung heroes—
ordinary people who make tremendous, if unappreci-
ated, contributions. Doug was just such an unsung
hero. He was an inconspicuous man who never
achieved anything outstanding on the job. Dependable, competent, and honest, Doug worked at a dairy.
He and his family lived in a comfortable home with a
beautiful vegetable garden.

Why, years after his passing, do many people remember Doug as one of their hometown's unsung heroes? Because he helped a number of boys through the
vulnerable years of adolescence—a time marked by
metamorphosis. Doug was a scoutmaster.

For most of his life, Doug was involved with the Boy
Scouts of America. The Boy Scouts have clearly defined requirements for boys who earn merit badges
and progress through the ranks. They encourage
achievement, personal growth, and character development.

Eagle Scout is the highest rank that a Boy Scout can
earn. There are no short cuts, and the requirements
are the same for the rich and poor alike. Every boy
can become an Eagle Scout. But he can't do it alone:
No youngster can achieve the personal growth, skill,
and character development this program affords, without people like Doug.

Doug took his scout troop camping on weekends and
during their summer vacations. Sometimes they fished
in the mountains. Other times, they camped out in the
foothills. Doug helped his scouts learn to build safe

campfires, how to cook, and how to hike through unfamiliar territory. During their weekly meetings, Doug made sure his scouts learned first aid and citizenship skills. He took them to the local pool and taught them swimming and life-saving skills. Doug was important in the lives of his scouts, augmenting the guidance and counseling they received from their families, teachers, and coaches.

No one was ever made to feel unwelcome in Doug's scout troop. He showed no favoritism and tolerated the boys' harmless rebellions. He instilled in them a sense of personal discipline by teaching them to obey the troop's rules. Doug helped guide many young men through the biological and emotional metamorphosis of adolescence.

Caterpillars become butterflies without external interference. Humans, like Mary Lennox and the other characters in *The Secret Garden*, need help from others to improve their lives. And that's why people in every community owe a great deal to men and women like Doug, the unsung heroes.

Reflections on
If It Weren't for Caterpillars,
There Wouldn't Be Any Butterflies

In the life of the butterfly, metamorphosis advances according to a predictable time schedule. The progress is generally the same for all butterflies; without intervention or opposition, they all achieve the same end— moving in a positive direction from ugly pest to beautiful pollinator.

For human beings, change is not totally predictable. It doesn't always progress in an orderly or convenient fashion. Unlike the one-way metamorphosis observed in insects, reversals in the human condition can and do occur. Just when you begin to behave as independent, fully functioning adults, you may revert back to childish behavior. You can lose skills that you previously mastered if you neglect them. And unlike a butterfly that does good but not harm, humans are capable of both good and evil.

Had her early childhood been happier, perhaps the fictional Mary Lennox would have been a lovable and charming young lady when she arrived at Misselthwaite Manor. And had it not been for Dickon's "supernatural" power over the robin that led Mary into the secret garden, she and several other characters would have remained in their miserable states.

Without men and women like Doug, whose accomplishments are in their service to others, none of us would ever realize our human potential. But with their guidance, we can reason and make choices during our own metamorphoses—the changes we experience.

Lessons Learned from
If It Weren't for Caterpillars,
There Wouldn't Be Any Butterflies

Change is exciting. Education changes us by releasing us from a prison of ignorance. Developing skills and abilities that enable us to make a living and interact effectively with other people also requires a metamorphosis. Here are some tips that may help you in your own metamorphosis:

• The first step in changing and progressing is to realize that both change and progress are possible. Most unrealized potential is the result of failure to try, not of failed attempts.

• Unlike insect metamorphosis, human metamorphosis is never complete. There is always more to learn and to achieve. So try to overcome habits, attitudes, and weaknesses that block achievement of your full potential.

• You can change your circumstances. If you dropped out of high school, you can go back and get your degree. If your grades were poor last semester, you can improve them in the current term. If you don't like your job, there are others to be had. If you have just received a poor performance appraisal, perhaps you ought to change what you do on the job.

• Some kinds of transformation require a good deal more personal effort than others.

• To resist change is natural, so if you get stuck, ask people you respect to help you get moving again.

• To take advantage of new opportunities, you often have to leave something behind. Just make sure what you leave behind isn't something you'll need in the future.

• The accumulation of a lot of little skills and the steady development of abilities makes you increasingly effective.

• Don't let people push you into trying to be someone you can't—or don't want to—be. Instead, rely on people whose goals for you are compatible with your goals for yourself.

• A penultimate thought on human metamorphosis: Mary Lennox illustrates a curious property of personal progress—you usually help yourself most when you are helping others.

• And last, people of achievement see opportunity and make the necessary personal change, or changes, to grasp it.

4

Experience Is What You Get When You Don't Get Your Way

"Can't I have just one more day to finish my report?"

"Come on, just a few more minutes and I can complete the test."

"But coach, I just ran two laps around the field. Why do I have to run another?"

"How come you're giving us homework this weekend? We have a school dance and we won't have time to study."

And so go the pleas so common to teachers and coaches.

"Look, I can't cut my budget any further and complete all the projects my unit has committed to this year."

"I know this is an important report, but can't it wait for a couple more days? I have to write performance appraisals that are past due."

"But boss, if you don't give me authorization to hire three more people this year, I can't do all the things you're asking of me."

And so go the pleas so common to business leaders.

In some cases, these pleas are based on fact. They may all be valid from the point of view of those uttering them. And they are neither right nor wrong. They spring from the need to avoid possible negative consequences. Whatever the response by teacher or coach or boss to these pleas, there are consequences for everyone involved.

Given unlimited time and resources, there is little that even the least talented or least ambitious person can achieve. But in school, at work, and in your personal life, you don't have unlimited time or resources.

Twice divorced and married for the third time, Beth had learned to cope with the pain and suffering produced by personal relationships in her early adulthood. She had married in her late teens, and had given birth to three children before divorcing her first husband and attending college. The divorce left her bitter. She swore never again to depend on someone else for financial support. A college degree would surely lead the way to well-paying jobs and financial security.

During the five years following her divorce, Beth worked as a waitress in the cocktail lounge of a big hotel. The pay was minimal, but the clientele tipped well. Combined with her student loan, income from the job was sufficient to pay the living expenses of her young family while she earned her bachelor's degree in business. Not having someone to help her with household chores placed an additional burden on Beth, but her drive and determination helped sustain her during late night and early morning hours of study.

Graduating summa cum laude, Beth applied for several entry-level professional positions at major companies in the area. Her interviews went well, or so she thought, but no jobs were offered. It was a slow time in the economic cycle, and companies weren't hiring external personnel to fill positions that internal candidates had worked hard to qualify for. Disappointed but not broken, Beth moved to a southeastern state to live with her grandparents for the short time it would take to find a good job there. As a trade-off, moving was a reasonable price to pay for admission to the ranks of up-and-coming business executives.

Packing up her family, Beth made the move and was soon hired as a credit analyst at a regional office of a major financial corporation. After a few short weeks of training, she engaged her work with the same dedication that had earned her high marks in college. Established in the initial phase of her career, Beth began to pay attention to her personal life. She had long been without male companionship, but now she met Phil, a co-worker. Not long after they began dating, Phil asked her to marry him and she accepted. Moving into a starter home in a new subdivision, Beth's children were thrilled to have a daddy living with them.

Beth's first two promotions weren't giant leaps to the top of the corporate world, but they signaled to Beth that her potential was being recognized by management. The next hurdle, to the ranks of management, didn't come so swiftly. There was a tremendous amount of competition for the few supervisory openings that occasionally became available. It took more than brains to win one of these positions. You had to have the right connections, and Beth was running behind her senior co-workers in that regard. Nonetheless, her ambition was unrelenting.

Beth began working very long hours. Bringing work home at night and spending Saturdays at the office took its toll on her relationship with Phil, and soon she was single again. It also exacted a price in the relationship with her three children, whom she neglected. Soon after her second divorce, they persuaded Beth to ask their well-established father if they could move in with him. Reluctantly Beth arranged for her children to live with their natural father and his wife in the northeast while the kids finished high school.

Now free from the demands of family, Beth tackled her job with increased fervor. She even earned an MBA from a university that had a weekend program. Still, it took two more years and a transfer to another location for Beth to become a manager. Unsatisfied with her deserved good fortune as a new member of management in a prestigious company, Beth wanted to outperform her peers. She was, moreover, a demanding subordinate to Jane, her boss. She constantly badgered Jane for more responsibility, more visible assignments, and more resources to get the job done. Furthermore, Beth didn't respond well to criticisms or suggestions. She was smarter and better educated than her boss, who had no college degree, and she wanted most of the credit for achieving positive results with projects that brought recognition. Recognition could result in promotions; and promotions meant greater success. To avoid confrontation with this "tiger," Jane capitulated to Beth's demands.

Managing a larger unit, Beth didn't change much, although she was a little happier because she had met John, whose ambitions paralleled her own. They both worked long, hard hours. Both were demanding subordinates, quick to criticize anyone in management who didn't see things their way and who failed to give them what they asked for or to provide the recognition they thought due them.

Business was booming for Beth's employer, a rapidly expanding company that now had more management positions than qualified, seasoned candidates to fill them. Beth was recognized as somewhat of a noisome manager, but she could get the job done—even though it usually cost more for her to do it than it should. So she was promoted to the ranks of middle management. She considered her new position a reward for her diligence and as proof that she was better than her competition. She had reached another rung on the ladder of corporate success. Little did she know what awaited her.

Tom was not exactly the kind of weak boss Beth was accustomed to. He was a hardened executive with many years of experience in handling subordinate managers and in meeting challenging assignments. Tom wasn't expected to be the next head of the division, but he was well-respected for his judgment and was thought by senior management to add tremendous value to the organization.

Beth was shocked by Tom's order to "cut the fat" from the budget for her new department. "What does he know anyway? This guy doesn't know it all. I'll beat him at his own game," she thought to herself. In their next budget and planning meeting, Beth presented Tom what he had asked for—a lean budget.

"Beth, I told you to cut the fat, not the projects. This plan is unacceptable. Let me tell you exactly what I expect from you," Tom said sternly.

Their relationship didn't improve over the next few months. Tom worked around Beth, who was acting like a spoiled child—pouting and griping. Beth, in turn, did all she could to soil Tom's reputation, tainting his department's reputation while she was at it. As a result, Tom gave Beth her first unsatisfactory performance appraisal. Furious, Beth went to Tom's boss to complain about his incompetence. "Do you realize what an arrogant ass he is to his staff? Are you unaware of the low morale in Tom's department? Tom is terrible to his people. He treats us like commodities and abuses us. He plays by his own rules and manipulates you and other senior managers. He never gives us what we need to get our assignments done. And he never shows any appreciation for our work!"

Blind to the years of association between Tom and his boss, Beth really expected the boss to ask Tom to step down and to then promote her to his position. Senior management would have to recognize how terrible an executive Tom was and how capable a replacement for him she was. Beth couldn't believe what she heard.

"I can understand that there may be some people who find Tom a difficult person to work for," said Tom's boss. "He is demanding, and not everyone is able to work for a person like him. But you need to recognize that we consider Tom to be the best executive we have ever had in his position, and we're behind him all the way. If you find working for him unbearable, my advice to you is to look for another job."

Her hearty appetite for success left no room for humility. Unwilling to work for Tom and get her job done effectively, Beth resigned in a fit of passion. Not surprisingly, her resignation eased tension for everyone affected by it.

Beth accepted a lower-level management position with a competing company and relocated once again. John, her third husband, was disgruntled because his career wasn't going anywhere, and he soon joined her in the new town. While she will most likely not be promoted to senior management in her new company, Beth has been able to implement some major cost-saving programs and so has been rewarded with big-number bonuses along with raises in salary. She's earning in total compensation about what she was making in salary while working for Tom, and she is well worth the money. Beth and John are happier now. They work hard, but don't live just for their careers. Beth has reconciled with her children, one of whom now lives with her and John. Although she would deny to her death that Tom ever taught her anything, Beth is considered by her new boss to be a solid manager. She has empathy for her staff, which goes a long way to earn their respect, and works hard under the pressure to lower operating costs. Moreover, Beth has developed tolerance for blindly ambitious subordinates who demand more resources or time than necessary to get their jobs done.

Reflections on
Experience Is What You Get
When You Don't Get Your Way

In school, at work, and in your personal life, it is very unusual to have all the time and resources you want to complete the task at hand. Doing your best is very frustrating when you "just know" more time will be required than has been allotted, when you "need" more resources to perform at your best, and when "no one" gives you the help you want.

You may quite naturally interpret not being given more time or more resources or more help as an absence of support from teachers, parents, friends, bosses, or associates. While you occasionally may be right that you need more support, this often is an erroneous assumption.

In business, for example, your boss probably receives competing requests for the same resources you want. A good manager handles such requests with circumspection and makes available additional resources to the subordinate managers whose work is most vital to the organization. The decision rarely seems fair to the subordinate who comes up short. Nevertheless, competent managers must know when to say no, whether or not doing so is comfortable for them.

The same principle applies in school. Teachers must set limits on how much time students have to complete tests and assignments. That is not to say that giving equal time to all students is always the best teaching technique. In a perfect world, students might be allowed all the time they need. In the real world, however, meeting deadlines can help you develop discipline and ingenuity. The ability to focus on the task at hand and get it done fast can separate the achiever from the also-ran.

Lessons Learned from
Experience Is What You Get
When You Don't Get Your Way

As Beth's experience illustrates, effort is not always rewarded. Furthermore, you don't always get your way even when its logic is obvious. Of course, you can blame others for your problems. You can fault your boss. You can fault your coach. You can fault your family and friends. You can fault co-workers. Blaming them is easy. But when you have finished finding fault, you have to make some tough decisions, take a few risks, and press on. Otherwise, you'll only be good at finding fault and placing blame. If you hang on to frustration and anger over apparent lack of support, you are in danger of carrying these emotions far into the future. Here, then, are a few of the lessons to be learned from experience:

• If each year of school were a repeat of the previous year, you'd never learn much. The same principle holds true at work. If each year is a repeat of the previous year, you're not going to grow much.

• Some students think they know more than their teachers, and unfortunately sometimes they do. However, an arrogant and ignorant student can benefit from a lesson in humility when the wise teacher calls on her or him to teach the class.

• Students can usually improve their grades and minds by going beyond the minimal requirements for passing the course. This is a good habit to form as a student because you acquire a self-discipline that can help you meet the challenges of your future career.

• Just as students in the same classroom don't profit equally from the experience, people in the same office gain varying degrees of insight.

• An education can provide you with skills and knowledge. Experience teaches you wisdom and judgment. And without wisdom and judgment, skills and knowledge have limited value.

• If you think the School of Hard Knocks is tough, consider how much harder it is for those without education than for those with it.

• Bright young subordinates sometimes think they know more than their more experienced bosses. They discover the flaw in this way of thinking when they begin to supervise subordinates who think they know more than the boss.

• When you are told no or to make do with what you have by your teacher or boss, grab the opportunity to learn a lesson that all successful people master: how to confront and manage adversity.

• Failure teaches you that you can't always count on winning. It provides you with a chance to learn how to deal with defeat. And it forces you to prepare to win the next time.

• People who make mistakes only once know how to learn from experience. Conversely, people who repeat the same mistake over and over again don't learn from experience.

• The most accomplished people in any profession make mistakes, are quick to admit them, and try not

43

to repeat them. In other words, they learn from their mistakes.

• Whenever you know how to do better than you're doing, do better—it helps you avoid lamenting later in life.

• Meeting arduous challenges gives you the self-confidence and insight needed by a top performer performing under pressure.

• Don't try to get more out of any given experience than it contains. And be aware when an experience contains few, if any, lessons of lasting value.

• Some lessons are comprehended long after the event that teaches them is over.

• And finally, successful people know it isn't important to get straight A's in all things, but they are willing to confront adversity to earn straight A's in important things.

5

If You're Never Afraid . . .
You Must Be Crazy

The Old Testament contains a fine story about not being afraid. It tells how a young shepherd, David, defeated an awesome warrior, Goliath, in battle.

To settle differences between two opposing forces in David's time, there were instances when a single champion from each army was chosen. These two met in combat, and the victor's army was declared the winner and gained all of the rewards of the conqueror.

Goliath of Gath was about nine feet, nine inches tall. In full battle dress his head was covered with a brass helmet. His body and legs were covered with a coat of overlapping brass scales that weighed over 150 pounds. Goliath's chest was also protected by a large breastplate of armor; his legs were encased in greaves of brass. He wielded a sword and a huge brass javelin. He was the champion of the Philistines, who had gathered their army to make war against the Israelites under the command of King Saul. The combative forces, in full battle array, were encamped on opposite hills separated by a valley.

On forty successive days, Goliath came down to the valley and called a challenge to the army of Saul: He would meet any Israelite warrior one-on-one to settle the conflict; this would spare other warriors from being killed in combat. But no man among the Israelites accepted the challenge. Terrified by the gigantic champion of the Philistines, the Israelites feared for their lives. Meanwhile, Goliath became more brazen in his challenge each day.

As it turned out, David had been sent by his father to check up on and carry provisions to his three older brothers who were in the army of Israel. After his arrival in his brothers' camp, David heard the challenge bellowed by Goliath. He didn't care much for the giant's defiance of the armies of Israel. David volunteered to do battle with the big oaf. He was immediately scolded by his oldest brother, Eliab, who said David was only a slight boy and not suited to defend the honor of their nation against such a formidable Philistine. Eliab then ordered his youngest brother to return to their father and tend their flocks. Instead, David went to King Saul and offered to take up the cause for the Israelites.

Saul advised David to consider his youth and inexperience, for Goliath was a proven warrior of many battles. David told his king that his God had helped him fight off wild beasts while watching his father's flocks, and Goliath was no more imposing

46

than any of these beasts. Surely his God would protect him, and he would slay the profane leviathan in combat. And so it was that Saul allowed this bold young man to defend the honor and freedom of his nation.

Refusing the armor that Saul offered him, David picked up five smooth stones from a brook and put them in a small bag that he wore around his waist. Armed only with these stones and his sling, David approached the Philistine. On seeing David, Goliath was angry that a mere boy had been sent to do battle with him—a boy armed only with a sling, a weapon used to chase away dogs, not a weapon of war. Goliath shouted to David that he was not only going to kill him but he was also going to feed him to the birds and the beasts. David yelled back to Goliath that with the help of his God, he, David, would surely triumph in their battle.

The one-on-one encounter was over almost as quickly as it had begun. David took one of the stones from his waist pouch, placed it in his sling, and hurled the stone into the unprotected forehead of the Philistine giant. Stunned, Goliath fell to the ground. Then David, using the giant's own sword, cut off his head. The battle-proven Goliath had not feared for his life, but was complacent in his belief that a shepherd boy without combat experience posed no threat.

No one expected Rick to have any concern about his future. He had just graduated with honors from one of the top universities in the country. Rick had been every professor's dream student. He attended every lecture, participated in class discussions, put in extra lab hours, handed in all homework assignments on time, and frequently visited his professors during their office hours to discuss their subjects as well as his own future plans. Rick had even studied in England one summer. Rick also wrote to titans of industry, to authors, and to publishers of business magazines to pose tough questions and asked for insights into his chosen career. His goal was to become a business leader, and the sooner the better.

It isn't difficult to understand his drive and determination once you learn a little about his past. Rick (his anglicized name) grew up in a country in the Far East that had an oppressive government. Intellectuals were sent to indoctrination camps where they could be reeducated in the philosophy of the ruling party. Acts of oppression flourished. All of this affected Rick directly. His father was sent to one of the reeducation camps; members of his extended family were sent to prisons, and some of them died or were executed during their incarceration. Rick grew up knowing real fear and tyranny. As a consequence, he developed a passionate desire to be free. He chose to use higher education as his passport to freedom in the Western world, and he was able to attend college in the United States.

Rick is not physically imposing, but he is impressive. Articulate, and well groomed, he has the manners of a diplomat. An engaging conversationalist, he listens as well as he speaks. Rick has involved many noteworthy people in his life and has single-handedly, through *chutzpah* and tenacity, organized a network of talented, experienced advisers for himself.

In keeping with his determination to gain a solid foundation for the leadership role he coveted, Rick turned down prestigious jobs and accepted a position in operations at a new organization. He wanted to learn the business from the bottom up. Rick was not crazy, but he feared going into something he knew nothing about. He wanted eventually to be a leader in the business world's high-risk environment, and he wanted to do well there.

Reflections on
If You're Never Afraid . . .
You Must Be Crazy

The problem with Goliath wasn't his lack of skills as a warrior. It was his failure to consider that a seemingly weak opponent could do him in. You'd think Goliath might hesitate to take on a naive shepherd boy at all. And you'd expect a seasoned warrior to wonder why the shepherd boy appeared on the battlefield without armor, shield, or sword—armed with only a slingshot. Goliath might at least scratch his head and pause, especially when the stakes were so high. After all, this battle would decide the outcome of a campaign between two warring nations. But the giant—surely the prebattle favorite in the eyes of any seasoned odds maker—had no trepidation. Perhaps Goliath really was a little crazy.

Rick is no Goliath. He has begun preparing himself for senior leadership in business. The road he has taken is not easy. In solving problems along the way, he will gain the knowledge, experience, and confidence necessary to play at high levels. His schooling and fine grades are impressive enough, but when you consider all of the extra preparations he has made to become a winner, you can see that Rick must be considered anything but crazy.

Lessons Learned from
If You're Never Afraid . . .
You Must Be Crazy

How comforting it is to realize that everyone has fears. From the straight A student to the high-school dropout, from the rich and famous to the poor and unknown, uncertainty, doubt, and worry are normal. Because it's okay to be afraid, consider these thoughts on dealing with fear:

• Not all your fears will be daunting. Some will be small and easily conquered. It is by conquering small fears that you become able to overcome greater ones.

• As a student, you will fear less those examinations that you have studied for than those for which you did not prepare. It follows that if you don't want to be afraid of tests, study for them.

• One thing you always ought to fear more than learning is ignorance.

• One of the most frightening days at work is a day on which your boss has scheduled a meeting with you to discuss your job performance and you know that you haven't done your best.

• Because you can't prepare for every possibility, there is no shame in being nervous in unfamiliar situations, but approach them in a measured, thoughtful way.

• From time to time, you'll find that being afraid of doing something is sufficient reason for avoiding it altogether.

• You become hostage to your fears when you don't confront them.

• Rich people may avoid taking risks for fear they'll lose their fortunes. But you often see people with little to lose taking large risks for large gains.

• The wisest among us understand that there are more important things to fear losing than money—like integrity, courage, confidence, the trust of others, and your own self-respect.

• Everyone has uncertainties, doubts, and fears to conquer. And it's always easier to understand and solve your own problems than someone else's.

• Fear failure less than you fear not enjoying the things you do well.

• Keep in mind that whenever you find yourself doing dangerous things with total disregard for their consequences, you probably are a little crazy.

6

Sometimes Life's Not Fair

"Puss in Boots" is an enduring fairy tale about a miller who left his mill to his eldest son, his donkey to his middle son, and his remaining possession, his cat, to his youngest son.

The youngest son felt unfairly treated. His two older brothers could work together using the mill and the donkey to make a living. But alas, left with only a cat, there was little hope for his own survival.

Hearing his new master's complaints, the cat asked him for a pair of boots and a sack. He told his master he would go into the bushes and return with many good things, proving that he, the cat, was not such a meager inheritance as the young man supposed.

Outfitted in his new boots and armed only with a sack, the cat made several trips into the woods where he captured various animals. Instead of returning to his master with his prey, the cat took them to the palace and presented them to the king in the name of his master, the "Marquis de Carabas." The cat repeated this scenario for several months, and all the while the king never realized there was no such marquis or that the cat's master was but the son of a dead miller.

The stage was now set. One day the cat instructed his master to bathe in the river at a spot he knew the king would pass with his daughter, the most beautiful princess in the world.

As the king's entourage approached the river where the miller's son was bathing, the cat yelled out for help, crying that his master, the Marquis of Carabas, was drowning. The king sent his guards to save the marquis. After the young man was "saved," the cat told the king that thieves had stolen his master's clothes while he bathed. So the king sent his servants to get clothing suited for a marquis.

As fate would have it—and after a little more deception and smooth talk on the part of the cat—the miller's son (now a marquis) married the king's daughter and became a wealthy man. So much for having been treated unfairly when his father divided his worldly goods among his three sons.

She had never been anything but trouble. Everyone thought she was dumb and lazy. She did poorly in school, and hung out with a rebellious crowd. She seemed doomed to a gloomy future.

Angelica, an only child, lived with her mother. They felt lucky to live in a small two-bedroom home just beyond "the projects" (a government-subsidized apartment complex on the city's east side where many of Angelica's friends lived).

Her teachers and most of her classmates thought Angelica was contentious, angry, hard to get along with, and destined for failure. They thought she couldn't care less about school, which was just a place she hung out until she could escape from it.

She belonged to "the pack," a group of kids who rarely completed homework assignments and did poorly on exams. "Angel," as she was known to her close friends, seemed to believe that anyone who took their schooling seriously didn't have a grasp on reality.

Because Angel was always causing disturbances, even her principal tried to avoid her. More than once, Angel carved her initials in a classroom desk. She carried a knife so big that not even her teachers dared stand in her way. Angel threw a lot of rocks during recess—sometimes at her classmates. She had a great arm and could have succeeded as a pitcher on the school's varsity baseball team.

If having a chip on the shoulder describes someone with a bad attitude, Angelica carried around a small tree on her shoulder.

Angel had never known her father. Her mother had moved to the city right after graduating from high school and wasn't on good terms with her own family. So Angel and her mother were in many ways alone and endured many hardships as a result. Angel and her mother were, in fact, fighting for survival.

T004089

Eventually Angel's high-school principal was forced to confront her as both a classroom disturbance and a potential danger to other students. But the undisciplined Angel refused to change. When her name was brought up before the disciplinary committee, neither Angel nor her mother showed up. The committee had little tolerance for such behavior. Angel was expelled in the middle of the tenth grade.

Angel's mother told her to get a job now that she wasn't going to high school. Angel didn't have any real interest in working, so she called her grandfather and asked if she could live for a while with him and her grandmother. Her mother grieved over losing Angel; nevertheless, she put her daughter on the bus and Angel was off to a small town in central Iowa.

The farmlands of Iowa were a tremendous contrast to the big city where Angel had always lived. The first thing her grandmother did was take Angel to the local department store and buy her clothes like those local teenagers wore. Angel thought, "Why not? I've zip to lose, even if the kids here are a bunch of hicks."

For the next five months Angel helped with chores around her grandparents' house, learning to milk cows and drive a small tractor. It was a real change of pace from her former life. Her grandparents introduced her to kids who lived on neighboring farms, but they were in high school and didn't have time to hang out. So to pass the time in the evenings, her grandmother encouraged Angel to read; there wasn't a whole lot more to do.

Summer came and Angel was able to spend time with kids her age. At first, they were suspicious of her. She spoke with a city accent and had dropped out of high school. But because no one expected her to be tough, and they all wanted to get to know her better, Angel tried to fit in. She went to Saturday-night dances and to a few sleepovers. The more she got to know Iowa farm kids, the more she liked them.

In the meantime, Angel's mother felt increasingly lonely. She had time to reflect on her past and on how much she missed her daughter. One evening when Angel called, her mother burst into tears. She told Angel how lonely she was and how much she wanted Angel to come home. Angel told her mother that she missed her too, but wasn't moving back to the city. Angel said things were different for her now, and she was just beginning to like herself. Similar telephone conversations continued during the next three weeks, until Angel finally decided to speak to her grandparents about her mother.

Openly, her grandparents told Angel they felt they had failed as parents. They hadn't been patient with Angel's mother during her teenage years, and she had grown rebellious and left town. For a long time, they hadn't known where she was, although they had reported her as missing. The police were unable to locate her. After seven long months, they had received a letter from her saying she was all right but intended never to return. There was no return address.

Now they assured Angel that they would welcome their daughter and welcome the chance to mend their relationship with her. Angel called her mother right away, and after three more telephone calls, her mother quit her job, packed up her meager belongings, and took a bus back to Iowa.

It was an intense reunion, with both tears and joy. During the weeks and months that followed, everyone worked to create a decent family life. Angel's mother got a job in town. Angel decided to go back to school in the fall, although she would be in tenth grade, and her classmates would be a year younger than she.

During the next few years, Angel fell in love frequently and temporarily lost her best friend, Kathy, because she won the heart of Kathy's boyfriend. The hostility didn't last long, and soon she and Kathy were on good terms once again. Angel's grades left a little to be desired. The fact that she had ignored her education for all of those years back in the big city made trouble now. But accepting tutoring and attending summer school between her junior and senior years enabled Angel to graduate from high school.

Meanwhile, her mother was seeing a childhood friend who had divorced some years earlier. After five months, they were married, and her mother moved into town with her new husband.

Angel stayed with her grandparents. She didn't

have any plans to go on to college. She didn't really know what she wanted to do. So she went to work at a plant that made breakfast cereal. Her job paid well and helped pass the time while she decided what to do next.

What she did next was marry. Angel met her future husband in the plant's parking lot. Several days later, when he hadn't invited her out, Angel approached him in the lunchroom and asked if he'd like to go to a movie. The rest was chemistry and rapport. They were married three months later.

Everyone loves a rags to riches story, but Angel's isn't one of them. She still works at the plant along with her husband. They have two children and live in a small home on four acres her grandparents gave them as a wedding present. They have never owned a new car, can't afford to travel, and have yet to mix with the social elite of their town. What they do have is basic happiness. They see their relatives often, have dependable friends, good jobs, and a nice vegetable garden. Each payday they set aside a little for their children's college expenses, and they manage to pay all their bills. It's a much better life than anyone ever expected for Angel, and no one should ever doubt that she has achieved success.

Reflections on
Sometimes Life's Not Fair

It doesn't take talent to inherit good fortune (with or without a cat's help). Talent comes into play when someone in poor circumstances improves their lot and when someone with every advantage creates an even better life.

The miller's son did end up with wealth and with the fairest princess in all the land. Perhaps some people think these things made him successful. Actually, it was the cat who was successful; the marquis just followed instructions.

Angel's success came from reversing the direction of her life and from promoting reconciliation between her mother and grandparents. She made many mistakes in her young life and had hard times. Angel never planned to escape from the ills of the city or even to graduate from high school. Her ability to improve her condition surfaced only after she was expelled from school and turned to her grandparents for help. Often the seeds of achievement are sown just when it seems as if circumstances couldn't get any worse.

Lessons Learned from
Sometimes Life's Not Fair

Life isn't always fair, and everyone has troubles and makes mistakes. Once you accept this truism, you are ready to consider your own personal achievements solely in the light of your own talents, abilities, and circumstances. Doing your best entails some bouncing back and not letting yourself be overcome by life's unfairness. Here are some thoughts on bouncing back:

• Straight A students may be excluded from the activities of peers who have lower grades. It's not fair, but accomplishment can elicit ridicule and jealousy that are hard to bear. Earning good grades and learning to endure ridicule and jealousy pays off later, however (whereas scorn of excellence doesn't).

• One of the best things you can do for other people is help them recognize how they can improve. This is especially true if you're a teacher or a boss and want your students or colleagues to strengthen their performances.

• If your problems are more than you can handle alone, you're wise to turn to someone who can help you work your way out of them.

• It is better to try one thing and succeed at it than to try many things and fail at all of them. The moment when you realize you're constantly failing, is precisely the moment when you ought to look for some small way in which to begin winning.

• Be thankful for and enjoy the success you have, but don't waste time lamenting the good fortune of others who have more.

• Seek your fortune and use it to help others instead of hoarding it for yourself alone. By the same token, if you use your talents selfishly, you'll never experience the joy that comes from sharing them with others.

• There are probably more happy and successful people who have modest incomes than there are happy and successful rich people. Remember that a sense of personal achievement is as difficult for the wealthy to achieve as for everyone else.

• High achievers who think they have made it on their own don't understand success. Your ability to succeed depends largely on how much help you've received from other people.

• When you rise to the top of your profession too rapidly, you fail to gain the circumspection and wisdom you need to remain there. Besides, some of the most successful people are not at the top of their professions. Rather their accomplishments lie outside their professions.

• In sum, life isn't always fair, some people have more talent and ability than others, some people have more money than others, and some people always seem to get the breaks. But everyone has problems, and people who learn how to solve them have the advantage over those who don't.

7

Guts and Grit
Never Hurt Anyone

The Odyssey is an epic poem written in the ninth century B.C. and attributed to the Greek poet Homer. In heroic verse, he tells the story of Odysseus's return home from the Trojan War—a bloody, ten-year conflict that originated in a dispute among three goddesses: Aphrodite, Athena, and Hera.

It all started at a wedding feast when Eris, or Strife, tossed a golden apple bearing the words *For the fairest* into the midst of the gods attending the wedding. Because all three goddesses claimed the apple, they asked Zeus to judge who among them was the fairest. Now Zeus was no dummy; he wasn't going to get involved in a bitter dispute among three gorgeous goddesses, so he told them that on Mount Ida they would find a certain shepherd, Paris, also called Alexander, who was an excellent judge of beauty and would make the right decision for them.

As it turned out, his ability to judge beauty was irrelevant. Rather than picking the fairest goddess, Paris chose the winner on the basis of the bribes the goddesses proposed to him.

Hera, as guardian of marriage, was highly regarded by married women; she, the sister and wife of Zeus, offered to make Paris the lord of Europe and Asia. Athena was a warrior goddess; she promised Paris that he would lead the Trojans into victorious battle against the Greeks and lay waste to Greece. Aphrodite, the goddess of erotic love and marriage, pledged to Paris that he could have the most beautiful woman as his own.

The result of the "Judgment of Paris" was that he gave the apple to Aphrodite as the most beautiful goddess. He wanted the fairest woman in the world.

The most beautiful woman in the world was Helen, who was actually the daughter of Zeus and Leda, a mortal. Helen was married to Menelaus. Before she had married, all of the young princes in the land had wanted her hand in marriage. Her father was believed by mortals to be Tyndareus, Leda's husband. He had been afraid that whoever married Helen would be attacked by the losing suitors. So he had persuaded all of the eager young princes to swear a solemn oath that they would come to the aid of Helen's husband if he was wronged through his marriage to her. After each man swore the oath, Helen was given in marriage to

Menelaus, the brother of Agamemnon and crowned king of Sparta.

Aphrodite knew Helen was the fairest woman in the world and that she was married as well. Bound by her promise to Paris, Aphrodite took him to Sparta, where he became a welcome guest of Menelaus and Helen. As the story goes, when Menelaus was away on business, he left Paris to care for his beautiful bride. And did Paris look after her! He seduced Helen in Menelaus's absence and took her back to Troy. On his return home, Menelaus found Helen gone and summoned all the princes bound by the oath demanded earlier by Tyndareus. He insisted they accompany him in making war on the city of Troy. Menelaus wanted his woman back.

Under the leadership of Agamemnon, the Greek princes assembled. As usual when war is declared, a few young men were reluctant to go. One of these was Odysseus. Odysseus had been warned by an oracle that if he went to war, he would be gone for twenty years. Therefore, he faked mental illness when the Greek princes came for him, assuming they would not want to go to war with a crazy man. But his deception was uncovered, and he was forced to go. So it was that an apprehensive hero, Odysseus, sailed with his army as part of the mighty Achaean expedition against the city of Troy. He was, as it turned out, on his way to a vicious war fought to return Helen to Menelaus.

As the *Odyssey* begins, Odysseus has been gone for about twenty years, just as the oracle predicted he would be. He has spent ten years in battle and ten more wandering the world, trying to return to Ithaca. The epic poem uses flashbacks to describe his trials and adventures during the latter decade. One obstacle after another prevents his reaching home.

For seven years Odysseus was held captive by the sea nymph Calypso, who wanted him to marry her. Although he was vulnerable to her enticements, he was faithful to his wife in that he refused Calypso's invitation to marry her.

He was also called on to lead his men past Scylla, a six-headed sea monster. Then there was the enchantress Circe. She turned his crew into pigs, but couldn't conquer Odysseus. After taking him as a lover, Circe helped Odysseus on his way. In another adventure, he used a little booze to numb the mind of, and a large spear to blind the eye of, a formidable foe. And so Odysseus escaped death at the hand of Polyphemus, a Cyclops who had held him and his men prisoner in a cave.

All the while, Poseidon, ruler of the sea, was mad at Odysseus and was responsible for a number of Odysseus's torments. Finally yielding to the collective desires of the other gods to let Odysseus safely return home to Ithaca, Poseidon eased off.

Odysseus returned to Ithaca, where he was king. There he was reunited with his wife (Penelope), his son, and his father. He punished those nobles who had tried in vain to woo and win Penelope while using his vast riches for their own pleasures during his absence.

• • •

Lloyd M. "Pete" Bucher was an orphan. He spent the earliest part of his childhood with his adoptive parents and their extended family. Enduring the hardships of poverty and a sometimes hostile environment, Pete became hardened at a young age.

After being apprehended for stealing fishhooks, Pete was sent to a reform school. The boys there were older and often abused him. Through the good efforts of the reform school administrators, he was then placed in the custody of a state-run orphanage in Boise, Idaho. Living with children his own age, he was better able to deal with his environment.

Over the next ten years, Pete sought relief from the tediousness of mediocre schooling by reading the books of such classic authors as Jules Verne, Daniel Defoe, and Robert Louis Stevenson. Just the same, he was not happy, for as the only Catholic in the orphanage, he didn't fit in. Pete endured the teasing as long as he could, then made a failed attempt to escape.

While planning his second escape from the orphanage, Pete learned that he was being transferred to a Catholic mission and orphanage in northern Idaho. No picnic awaited him there, either.

Pete earned better than average grades from the Catholic Sisters of St. Joseph. The nuns made him earn his keep by performing various farm chores, but Pete still found time to read every book available to him in the library. Reading the sports pages of old newspapers and seeing that wonderful old movie (starring Spencer Tracy and Mickey Rooney) about Father Flanagan's Boys Town of Nebraska fed his longing to play football with other boys—and to live at Boys Town.

Through a series of lucky events, Pete did indeed gain admission to Boys Town. There, under the influence of good and encouraging men like his coach Skip Palrang, Pete developed strong character. The stern teacher-priests who enforced the school's strict code of conduct and discipline also left a lasting imprint on him. Pete became a regular starter on the football team, which he eventually captained. In 1946, he graduated among the top ten in his class. Pete's sense of duty led him to the nearest navy recruiting station. A two-year stint in the navy was as far into his future as he could see.

When his two years in the navy were over, he joined the navy reserves. He used the GI Bill and a partial football scholarship to attend the University of Nebraska. He remains, to this day, a devout fan of Nebraska football.

On June 10, 1950, Pete married Rose Dolores Roling, a magnificent woman from Jefferson City, Missouri. Then shortly after conflict broke out in Korea, the navy began to call up its reserve forces. Pete, a petty officer first class, was among those recalled.

Determined to complete college, as well as to serve, he applied for and was accepted in a modified Reserve Officer's Corps candidate program. His recall orders were amended to allow him to attend two six-week navy sessions during the next two years while he completed his education.

Eventually returning to naval service, Ensign Bucher gained further recognition when he was one of a very few non-Annapolis graduates accepted into the elite submarine officer's training school.

Over the next few years, every time Pete and Rose considered a return to civilian life, an international conflict developed that might indicate the recall of reserve officers. Not wanting to leave naval service just to be called back—and after discussions with Rose—Pete applied for recognition as a regular naval officer. He would now make a career of the navy.

A disarmingly forthright man, Pete Bucher never had ambitions to rise to the top ranks in the navy. But he served diligently in all his assignments. Meanwhile, periods of prolonged absence from his family tested his relationship with Rose; nonetheless they had a good life with their two fine sons. The Buchers were and are a family who stick together.

In December 1966, Lieutenant Commander Lloyd M. Bucher, USN, was stationed at a U.S. Seventh Fleet base out of Yokosuka, Japan, where he was serving as assistant operations officer of Submarine Flotilla 7. One morning he was handed orders to proceed to fleet headquarters in Hawaii. As the prospective commanding officer of AKL 44, he was to attend briefings on the top secret Operation Clickbeetle.

Operation Clickbeetle was the code name for a program of electronic and radio intelligence gathering by small, unarmed ships operating near potential enemies of the United States. AKL 44 was one of four small surface ships to participate in this intelligence-gathering program.

Pete was a submarine officer. His new orders were bringing him to the surface. In the minds of the naval elite—submariners—Pete had just been traded from the major leagues to the minor leagues.

Although he was not overjoyed with his orders, Pete managed to sound excited when he called Rose to tell her of his new assignment. After all, being named the commanding officer of any ship is no small distinction in the navy.

In time, as one event led to another, Pete eventually captained the lightly armed USS *Pueblo* as she sailed to her primary area of operation—the Sea of Japan, just beyond the territorial waters of North Korea.

January 23, 1968, was to be one of the final days of Commander Bucher's intelligence-gathering mission. Soon he would head back to port. The seas were swelling; water was freezing on the ship's deck; for their own safety, Pete ordered everyone to remain inside for the day.

At his initial sighting of a North Korean submarine chaser approaching the *Pueblo* at flank speed, Pete recalls being more annoyed than alarmed. But as the ship continued toward them, he hurried below to confirm that his ship was "legal" (in international waters). Lying dead in the water 15.9 miles off the island of Hung Do, Pete had no doubt that the *Pueblo* was completely legal.

The situation deteriorated fast. Pete's protests to the approaching Russian-built SO-1 class submarine chaser were ignored and the harassing ship was joined by others: Soon the *Pueblo* was encircled by six North Korean naval ships. Intensifying the danger, two North Korean MiGs began to circle overhead. The Korean ships opened fire, shooting one to two thousand machine gun rounds, and six to fourteen cannon shells at the *Pueblo*. Commander Bucher and eleven of his crew were wounded. The *Pueblo* was seized and all but one of its men taken prisoner by the North Koreans. Fireman Duane Hodges died from wounds incurred during the attack.

During the eleven months of their captivity, Commander Bucher, his officers, and crew received barbaric beatings regularly. They were also subjected to mental torture. By any standard, they were fed poorly. And medical treatment wasn't forthcoming until shortly before their release; even then, it was inferior.

Released by North Korea with his junior officers and crew in December 1968, Pete was far from free. He was brought before a navy court of inquiry, a grand jury of sorts. The court recommended that Commander Bucher be tried by general court-martial for alleged offenses under the Uniform Code of Military Justice that led to the *Pueblo*'s capture and other violations of conduct as her commanding officer. Overruling the recommendation of the court of inquiry, Secretary of the Navy John H. Chaffe ordered the charges against Commander Bucher dropped. Without speaking to Commander Bucher's guilt or innocence, Secretary Chaffe stated, "They've suffered enough."

Pete served a few more years in the navy. After his retirement, he was accepted by the Art Center College of Design in Los Angeles. Not an easy school to get into, it customarily accepts only students who have already earned an art degree. After twelve months of studying, Pete left the school and began to draw professionally. He's been a commercial artist ever since.

On May 5, 1990, Commander Bucher and sixty-three of the seventy-nine *Pueblo* crew members who are still alive were honored at a modest ceremony in San Diego, where they were awarded Prisoner of War Medals. Even then, twenty-two years after the *Pueblo* incident, the self-protective navy, which had wanted to make Commander Bucher the scapegoat, fought to block the award. But the medals awarded the men of the *Pueblo* had been specifically ordered by Congress.

Reflections on
Guts and Grit Never Hurt Anyone

As *The Odyssey* illustrates, to achieve your goal, you sometimes have to have a large measure of guts and grit: simple perseverance. Odysseus's number one goal was to return home. Along the way he met numerous obstacles, any one of which could have spelled failure. His courage and strong sense of responsibility, however, kept him going.

Odysseus was the first of the Greek epic heroes to have both brain and brawn. A shrewd warrior, he used his brain to reason before engaging his brawn. Odysseus was also reputed to be a cunning and wily character (one of his slaves describes him as "a lying, pitiless lord"). And as is the case with many heroes, his prime weakness was his overbearing pride. But Odysseus was not a quitter.

Pete Bucher has experienced many difficulties. Against all odds, he graduated from high school. He graduated from college. He earned a commission in the U.S. Navy. He married well. He never shirked his duty to his country. Although illegally imprisoned and mercilessly beaten, he survived. His wife and his sons stood by him even when the country seemed, for a time, to be embarrassed by what Pete was caught doing—what he had been sent by his government to do.

Pete never lost faith in his country. More than two decades after the *Pueblo* incident, he went to bat for his crew—against the navy—so they would be recognized for the sacrifice they had made for their country.

A man with a charming sense of humor, Pete has both his feet firmly on the ground and his head squarely on his shoulders. He, like Odysseus, is a man of reason. Although he considers himself anything but a hero, Pete is a brave, responsible man. He has no lingering bitterness about the burdens he has had to shoulder. Nothing was ever given him, but he never gave up. Pete Bucher has earned every measure of success granted him.

Success isn't a prize that you win—it must be earned. If you want to make something of yourself, no matter what hand you have been dealt, you must have faith in yourself and play your hand realistically. You will always face uncertainty. You will have both real and imagined doubts and fears to conquer. And you will find that very often, success comes to those who persevere and never give up.

Lessons Learned from
Guts and Grit Never Hurt Anyone

In a world where so many good things are instantly available, success is neither instant nor always available. You can only achieve what you earn. In the process of earning the success and happiness you seek, you'll make mistakes. You'll stumble over obstacles in your path. Sometimes those you trust will trip you up. The realization that success is earned—plus the ability to cope with everyday challenges—contribute to life-long personal achievement. Here are a few thoughts that may help you on your journey:

• One of the worst mistakes you can make is to tell yourself (or to believe someone else who tells you) that you'll never amount to anything.

• You will, sooner or later, be held hostage by your past or your present. To achieve anything of note you must then find the personal courage to break out of this artificial jail.

• Your ability to overcome difficulties is partially governed by your refusal to let them keep you down.

• Stamina, will, courage, and faith in yourself separate winners from losers.

• Not having the courage to overcome daily trials is more tragic than failing to achieve all the greater success of which you're capable.

• If you want to fail badly enough, you can always find a reason for not living up to your potential.

• The only loneliness greater than the loneliness of failure is the loneliness of those who lose their ambition to overcome their failure.

• If your only ambition in life is to acquire material wealth, be prepared to pay a heavy personal price.

• If you work hard all your life and acquire few material things, remember that being poor is a state of mind—it has nothing to do with money. There are happy, successful people who have very little money, and there are unhappy, unsuccessful rich people.

• Not even the desperation and fear we all feel at one time or another should move you to lie, cheat, steal, manipulate, or use duplicity to achieve your goals.

• Success involves a process whereby you are inspired to fulfill your true potential. And the extent of your full potential is never absolutely known.

• Last, role models serve as a source of inspiration, but remember that role models commit errors. Moreover, they once needed strong role models of their own.

8

So . . . You Think You're the Only One Who Has Problems?

An enterprising television producer created a new game show thinking it could capture a wide viewing audience and perhaps even the number one rating for its time period.

Its creator thought the game show would demonstrate that no matter how terrible your own personal problems are there is always someone else who has worse ones. To a limited degree, the show would serve as mass psychotherapy by helping a large number of people put their personal problems in perspective. This aspect of the game would provide the show with more than just entertainment value for its audience.

The game would be played by four principal contestants. Prior to the show, members of the studio audience would anonymously submit their most formidable problems, which could be related to finance, jobs, family, personal relationships, or health.

A member of the show's staff would put twenty of the problems on a list to be passed out to the studio audience. The studio audience would rank the problems from one to twenty, with twenty indicating the most terrible problem. A game show statistician would then assign a number from one to twenty to each of the day's problems. The problems and their assigned numbers would be shown to the studio and viewing audiences, but not to the contestants.

At the start of the show, each contestant would be given a bankroll of $5,000. The contestants would take turns spinning a wheel with one outwardly pointing arrow affixed to a disk with letters on the rim. When the wheel stopped, the arrow would point to a letter identifying a window on a gigantic board. Behind each of the twenty windows would be one of the day's problems. The windows would be curtained, and no one would be able to see what problems were concealed until the end of the show. A contestant could "buy" a window for $100 or pass. If the contestant passed, the other contestants could bid for that window. The bidding for each window would continue until no other contestant raised the last bid. Contestants could not bid more than they had in their bankrolls. If no contestant bid for a window, it would become a "lost opportunity." This process would be repeated until time ran out or until all contestants had spent their bankrolls. The contestants would be challenged to buy as many windows as possible, hoping that theirs would be the worst problems of the day and would, therefore, have the highest values.

At the end of the show, the curtains would be removed to reveal both the problems and their numbered values. The amount paid by each contestant for each window would be multiplied by the number assigned to that problem. Windows that had been passed would be given a value of $750 each. The contestant with the largest final number would become the champion. However, the champion wouldn't necessarily win any money. To merit a prize, his or her score would have to be higher than the total score of the windows no one had bid on. If the champion's score was less than the score of the unbought windows, the champion, like the three other contestants, would receive no cash prize.

Confident that her show would be a big hit, the producer presented the idea to the network's executives. Alas, the show never was produced because the executives didn't think anyone would be interested in other people's problems.

A few years ago, Marta and Alexia were two college students who worked as summer waitresses at the lodge that overlooks the North Rim of the Grand Canyon. They were roommates in the women's dormitory.

Marta was from a university in Idaho. She had been raised on a potato farm there and had lived in a small town all her life. Her parents earned a good living on the farm but were not rich. Alexia was from a private college in southern California. She had been born and raised in the Los Angeles area. Her father was a self-made man who had earned considerable wealth in his construction supply business. Her mother sold real estate and made a lot of money, too. The two young women became summertime friends.

Marta talked to Alexia about school, about life back home in Idaho, and about the men she dated at college. Marta was a good student but had never made the honor roll. She was still learning about life outside Idaho.

Alexia was rather sophisticated. She received straight A's in both high school and college. She looked like a fashion model but never acted as if she were superior to her roommate. She listened to whatever Marta had to say but didn't talk about her own life.

One time Marta pressed Alexia about the men in her life, and Alexia said she didn't date much. "There is something about me that gets in the way of any boy taking a serious interest in me. Perhaps we can talk about it another time." Not wanting to pry further, Marta dropped the subject and never brought it up again.

As the end of the summer neared, Marta promised to stay in touch with Alexia. Marta had learned a lot from Alexia, who seemed mature beyond her years. She had always listened to Marta's problems and questions, and had helped her grow in many ways. For instance, Alexia was a geology major and could read the canyon's history in its rock formations. Her hikes in the canyon with Alexia on their days off were a highlight of the summer for Marta. Marta thought she and Alexia would always be special friends.

In general, when people work together in temporary situations, they form close but ephemeral relationships. Marta and Alexia were no exception. They had exchanged both their college and home addresses and telephone numbers, but they only wrote each other twice before they got caught up in college activities and soon after stopped corresponding altogether.

Two years later, Marta and a college friend went to Disneyland for spring break. It was Marta's first trip to California. Because Alexia lived in southern California, Marta called her home from the motel.

A girl answered—probably one of Alexia's younger sisters. "Is Alexia there?" Marta asked.

A moment of silence was followed by the sound of a young girl crying. The receiver was dropped, perhaps on a table or countertop. Marta couldn't quite make out the conversation being conducted near the phone.

"Who is calling? Why are you asking for Alexia? Is this a cruel joke?" demanded the woman who picked up the receiver.

Marta replied in dismay, "My name is Marta. Perhaps Alexia has told you about me. We were roommates two summers ago at the Grand Canyon. I'm in the area for spring break and just wanted to see how Alexia is doing."

"Please accept my apology. Your call really upset

my youngest daughter, and I thought you were a prank caller," the woman responded. "You see, three years ago Alexia became very ill and we almost lost her. Then she recovered for a while. That was when she went to work at the Grand Canyon. Last December her leukemia came out of remission and Alexia passed away."

Reflections on So . . . You Think You're the Only One Who Has Problems?

It is not uncommon for someone with problems to become self-centered and have little interest in other people's problems. Teachers can become so focused on administrative and policy issues that they pay little or no attention to the problems in their classrooms. Bosses can be so caught up with corporate challenges that they have no time to help subordinates solve problems that may be even more important to the organization. And so, as the network executives who turned down the idea for the game show understood, both teachers and bosses can operate on the principle, "I don't have time for your problems, I have too many of my own."

Appearances are often deceiving. Many students who receive high marks in school are envied by peers who believe that straight A's come naturally to them. Popular students are thought by others to have few, if any, problems getting dates. Flawed perceptions can lead students to think that rich kids have no worries. And altogether too many adults never outgrow false notions about other people's problems.

Alexia was bright, pretty, talented, and rich. She seemed to Marta to have no problems at all. Yet Alexia had a fatal illness she could do nothing about. Rather than choose to suffer, Alexia lived as if nothing were wrong (except that she avoided becoming involved with boys because she doubted there was a future for such a relationship).

Few personal problems have a fatal ending. Most can be resolved. Always keep this in mind—especially when a new and unusual problem crops up.

Lessons Learned from So . . . You Think
You're the Only One Who Has Problems?

Every time you solve a problem, you learn from it. You also learn by helping other people solve their problems. Learning to solve problems is one of the competencies you begin developing in your school days and continue to develop throughout your adult life. It doesn't matter if yours are the world's worst difficulties. There is no prize to win even if they are. What matters is that you don't become excessively anxious—which becomes another problem for you to solve—that you don't let your problems persist for too long over time, and that you try to solve your problems without overburdening other people.

• Dealing directly with problems isn't always easy. Sometimes there are no simple solutions.

• By encouraging students to overcome difficulties,

teachers not only help them in the present, but also help society avoid problems in the future.

• There are many things that you may see as problems that, redefined, are not problems at all.

• You should always deal with problems head-on. But don't let problems become your reason to live unless you want to become a martyr.

• In those situations where you aren't able to solve a problem facing you, ask for help. In asking for help, be sure to ask someone who might be able to help.

• On one of those days when you don't seem to have a problem or a care in the world, enjoy yourself. It won't be long before your life returns to normal.

• Much of the stress you experience may be created by recognizing a problem and doing nothing about it.

• Some people are constantly looking for problems and conflict. These are people you ought to avoid.

• As a boss, whenever you help subordinates solve problems that are beyond their abilities, you accomplish at least two things: teaching the subordinates and resolving problems before they become bigger issues.

• Any time bosses find out that their subordinates are reluctant to bring problems to their attention, the bosses ought seriously to consider changing their own behavior, because it has led to this organizational problem.

• And finally, education and training can prepare you to make important career decisions. But even so, the journey down the path to any good and worthy goal is rarely, if ever, without mishap.

9

Survival of the Fittest

The phrase *survival of the fittest* is often attributed to Charles Darwin, the nineteenth-century English naturalist. But Darwin's actual phrase, used in connection with his theory of natural selection, was *survival of the fit*. Darwin, by the way, incorporated ideas of Herbert Spencer and at least two other naturalists in his theory of natural selection.

Today, Darwin's ideas are often misinterpreted to equate the *fittest* with the *mightiest*, the *most magnificent*, or the *most praiseworthy*. Darwin, however, used *survival of the fit* to refer to individuals who reproduced and in so doing enabled themselves to survive long enough to produce offspring. Nothing in Darwin's theory justifies claims to elitism or dreams of a superior race.

A common belief today is that the ability to adapt

is the essence of survival of the fit. The course of adaptation can be influenced by many extraneous factors. For instance, hybridization, deliberate control of reproduction, and gene splicing can impact the ability of organisms to adapt and, therefore, to survive.

Adaptability is significant in a daily (nonevolutionary) sense, too. Your ability to adapt influences where you live, where you work, what career you choose, whether or not you marry, whom you marry, whether or not you remain married, whether or not you have children, how many children you have, how much education you gain, and so forth. It even affects your emotions and attitudes and the way you approach or avoid certain people and situations.

Julie was an average student. She didn't like science and mathematics, but she was keen on the social sciences, the humanities, and physical education. Her family lived in a lower-middle-class neighborhood. Both her parents worked at semiskilled jobs, and her four siblings shared routine family chores with her.

Perhaps it was the sparkle in her eye or her enthusiasm in group activities that made Julie popular with her classmates. She was, quite simply, a joy to be around. Julie seldom seemed discouraged; only infrequently and briefly did she get down on herself. Active in student government and in extracurricular activities, she played on the girls' basketball team.

She also dated popular guys. Julie was well liked by her teachers, although she needed tutoring to maintain her C average. Luckily, her teachers were glad to provide her with extra help.

A corporate career wasn't an adolescent fantasy of Julie's. She could see only as far ahead as college and didn't know yet what her major would be. Her high-school grades and her scores on the Scholastic Aptitude Test were less than distinguished but did allow her to attend a small state college in the Midwest.

A B average student in college, Julie joined a sorority and was active in the college's Greek community. Her professors were attracted to her enthusiasm for life and gave her extra help when she floundered academically. Encouraged by several professors who recognized both her ability to get along with other students and to organize campus activities, she chose a major in business management.

Shortly before graduation, one of Julie's professors was contacted by a former student who had become a middle manager in a pharmaceutical company. He was recruiting for a management intern position. The professor recommended Julie.

Julie had never before considered working for an international pharmaceutical company. Nor had she ever expected to move to New Jersey, which is where the company's corporate headquarters was. Nonetheless, she was soon established in her own apartment in New Jersey. During her internship, she learned technical terminology and company policies, she figured out who was who in the organization and how to get things done, and she discovered what senior management expected from her.

In the next few years, Julie traveled internationally, met a wide array of customers, and attended many conventions and trade shows. What she lacked in academic intelligence and technical aptitude she compensated for with her ability to get colleagues to help her master details about the nature and benefits of the company's product line. Her keen ability with people paid off, and she often attended meetings with senior management, who took a real liking to her.

When Julie became sales manager for the Dallas area, she achieved record sales. In her next position, as sales director for the western region, Julie's business results were the best in the company. As a consequence, she was transferred back to corporate headquarters in New Jersey as vice-president of domestic sales. She bought a handsome townhouse in an up-scale area and renewed friendships from her previous years in New Jersey.

Along the way, Julie surpassed, in both promotions and pay, peers who were more technically competent than she. She outperformed several graduates of prestigious business schools. Accepting new positions in distant cities wasn't always easy, although each move was accompanied by a promotion and a salary increase. For moving is upsetting even for people like Julie. Moreover, her promotions weren't swift and she wasn't on the fast track. It took her a while to gain expertise, but once she learned something, she remembered it and applied it on the job.

Julie is not expected to be promoted to the next higher level of management. She could have accepted one of several offers of higher positions in smaller companies. But she likes where she is and what she is doing. And she is comfortably raising her two children with her husband, a pharmacologist at the same company.

Not the best, not the brightest, not the toughest— Julie is representative of many executives in corporate America where adaptability—survival of the fittest—holds attractive rewards. Stories like Julie's are repeated often not only in business but also in government, small business, and education where adaptability is a way of life.

Reflections on
Survival of the Fittest

Julie was successful because she made conscious choices about how to allot her time and how to use her talents at work.

It was to Julie's advantage in both school and in her career that she was adaptable. She also benefited from receiving extra help and encouragement from both her teachers and her business colleagues. From them she gained insight and wisdom that she never would have acquired on her own.

All through life, you need to adapt not only to survive but also to thrive. Many events require adaptability: taking a new job, making friends, losing a friend or loved one, getting married, bringing a child into the world, relocating, going to college, joining the military, playing on athletic teams, working for a new boss, hiring a new subordinate. All these and many other challenges demand adaptability on your part. And adaptability was the crucial ingredient in Julie's success.

Lessons Learned from
Survival of the Fittest

Being too anxious to realize your dreams, too eager to move on to the next challenge, too determined to have things your way can be counterproductive. The simple truth is that you can't have it all. Trade-offs are necessary. You have to give up good options and pass up appealing opportunities when you make wise choices about what you want and what you will do to get it. You will be forced to adapt in order to progress. The following thoughts may be useful in making decisions and developing adaptability:

• Teachers are similar to bosses: You rarely get to choose them; some are good and some are bad. And while you're subject to their authority, what they think of you really does matter.

• Adapting to rules you object to at school won't make you a good student, but it will eliminate difficulties you'd otherwise encounter.

• Life is full of rules, so learn to follow them or to work within bad rules until they can be changed. Breaking rules is a bad habit that rarely has any positive outcome or lasting reward. The most successful people see situations clearly and change them, if necessary. People who act according to what they think the rules should be instead of according to what the rules are usually fail. But, sometimes rules must be broken to achieve personal progress. So when you break the rules, make certain the rules you are breaking won't break you.

• No one thrives under any and all conditions. Therefore, select friends, work, recreation, and the place you live so that they bring out the best in you. This may take more than a little courage, for making the right decisions may involve making major changes in your life.

• Don't expect other people to always adapt to you. If you are going to fulfill your dreams and ambitions, you will have to make some accommodations in your own thinking.

• Being adaptable doesn't mean compromising your values. Nor does it mean being spineless. A little inflexibility is a good characteristic.

• Adapting won't always change things for the better nor improve the odds for your surviving among the fittest. Hold your ground when necessary.

• Take advantage of any opportunity to become more effective. Accepting good advice from teachers, peers, friends, and family can be profitable. So can observing the ways in which they adapt to circumstances successfully.

• Career goals are useful, but if climbing the ladder of success is your only ambition, you're headed for emotional extinction. Why? Because success and happiness come from more sources than just your job. And because you can never control or adapt to all the variables in your career. To some extent, career success depends on being in the right place at an opportune time.

• Be patient in waiting for opportunities that are right for you to present themselves. In the meantime, gain all the knowledge, experience, and wisdom you can. These will help you become more successful and may even help you make better decisions for yourself.

• Many rewards are acquired by enduring your surroundings and circumstances long enough to work through and master their inherent difficulties.

• If your goal is to climb the ladder of success, knowing when to adapt to various situations will improve your chances of getting there.

• Setting only one goal and placing many conditions on success won't allow you to adapt to the difficulties and failures you'll meet.

• And last, stand up for your ideals and look after your own best interests. You can and should set high standards of achievement for yourself. You needn't and shouldn't sell out. Achievers are often tough, powerful, rich, and intelligent. They should also be honorable.

10

Report Cards
Get an F

Throughout the ages, both civilized and developing societies have been obsessed with measuring individual abilities competitively.

The Greeks held contests to discover who could run the fastest, heave metal objects the farthest, jump the highest, and pin another's shoulders to the ground the quickest. The Romans held chariot races and a few Christian-eating contests for their pet lions. Native Americans raced horses and pitted their warriors against one another in contests to see who could shoot arrows the farthest and who had the truest aim throwing the tomahawk.

In this age, the twilight of the twentieth century, enterprising officials of the National Basketball Association have created a competitive match to determine who can slam-dunk the ball the best. Never mind that in basketball a slam dunk counts for only two points however stunning a player's maneuver to the rim. But for rabid fans, the physical prowess with which points are scored is sometimes more important than whether their team wins or loses.

On it goes, man's obsession with competition— some of it banal and having little purpose beyond competition for competition's sake. Meanwhile, the more vital form of competition—one's performance as measured against one's own potential—goes largely unnoticed.

In small towns across the country, local boys race family cars against pickup trucks to establish who rules the road. Others compete for hunting rifles awarded by local hardware stores to whoever bags the biggest buck during deer-hunting season. Every autumn at county fairs, blue ribbons are given to whoever has grown the best vegetables; created the tastiest jams and jellies; raised the choicest lambs or calves, the fattest pigs, the finest goats, the most outstanding chickens; or stitched the most fetching quilt.

It follows that as a student you become competitive. One of the earliest forms of competition you encounter involves measuring yourself against other students on the time-honored scales of academic proficiency. Your standing as a student is reflected on report cards.

Academic performance may partially reflect the quality of a child's upbringing, and so parents sometimes boast of their offspring's good grades, as if these grades predicted nonacademic achievement as well.

No matter where you live, at almost any social function, you are likely to hear at least one conversation about how much someone else's child enjoys school, gets along with his or her classmates, and likes the teacher. The boasting parent often announces that his or her child is at the head of the class, as confirmed by the latest report card. Sometimes you just can't deny the effects of good breeding.

For such insecure adults, the accomplishments of their children are direct manifestations of their own success as parents and providers. And, by confirming that their own student is progressing better in school than his or her peers, the insecure confirm that they are, after all, more able as parents and providers than their friends and neighbors.

"Let me tell you about Malcolm. What an amazing child. He is captain of his soccer team and scores an average of five goals a game. Of course, he could score more often, but his coach has him play goalie during the second half. He is so good at that too. Why, no one has yet to score on him. In scouts, he has completed every requirement to qualify as an Eagle Scout. He just has to be patient until the badges are awarded. You see, he is only eleven, and there is an age requirement for earning the Eagle Scout rank.

"Just last week he had a recital at the conservatory and played Mozart and Chopin. Everyone was amazed. You see, he didn't require any sheet music. Malcolm always plays from memory.

"He is so popular that last year he was unanimously elected president, vice-president, and secretary at school. The principal told us it was the first time in the school's history that one child was elected to every office simultaneously.

"His teachers look up to him. He gets 100 percent on every test. Malcolm really is special. Just for fun, he took organic chemistry and cultural archaeology at the university last summer.

"He reads every night before he goes to bed. Last week he read *The Complete Works of William Shakespeare*. This week he says he is going to buzz right through *The Story of Civilization* by the Durants. Malcolm hardly has time to go swimming and fishing, to watch MTV, or play with his friends. Besides, he says his friends are boring."

If you have any doubts about the validity of such common stretching of the imagination, just remember holiday newsletters from friends. Sometimes such boasting and exaggeration makes you wonder what will happen if these children fail to live up to their parents' expectations or, for that matter, what's left in life for them. The poor kids might as well move to Florida and take up shuffleboard.

If your child is "just" average, how can you compete? You've lost from the outset. Surely your average child will never amount to more than average as an adult. If your child is below average, there may be no hope at all. Right? Wrong! Rest assured, this line of thinking is utter nonsense!

The bus ride to San Diego was long, hot, and tiring for Charles, who was called "Spike" by his close friends. It was his first journey beyond his hometown.

On the trip he envisioned himself in the dress blues of the U.S. Marine Corps—the subject of photo opportunities for thousands of visitors who would snap his picture as he stood guard at the Tomb of the Unknown Soldier.

The gunnery sergeant (gunny) who enlisted Spike into the marines had assured him that his lack of a high-school diploma wouldn't be a factor in his service. Boot camp would turn him into one of the special few— the proud and the brave. He would become a marine! Drill instructors would teach him all he needed to know, they would look out for his welfare; he would become part of the elite team—the U.S. Marines. "Trust me, boot camp will be an experience that you'll never forget. Congratulations and good luck," were the last words the gunny spoke to Spike as the young man kissed his loving mother good-bye and boarded the bus that would carry him to a place where his life would be forever changed.

Spike was rudely awakened to the harsh reality of boot camp as he stepped off the bus at the Marine Recruit Training Depot, San Diego, to a cacophony of incoherent orders, shouted from the lips of "kind and friendly" drill instructors who "warmly" welcomed him and his cohorts to their new home. His hair would be shaved from his head in short order—with less finesse than sheep were sheared back home. For the next few months, he would march double time in formation everywhere he went.

In the chow hall, Spike scarfed down meals meant only to keep his stomach from eating his backbone. "We're here to make marines out of you bums, not to fatten you up," the boot camp cadre reminded Spike and his fellow recruits. Training was more important than eating.

Spike was expected to make his rack (bed) to exacting standards every morning—a quarter dropped on it had to bounce back at least twelve inches or his gunny would tear his rack apart, give him an order to perform some personal-incentive physical training exercises (push-ups), and let him try making his rack again. It seemed a strange custom and surpassed anything his mother had ever demanded from him. Boots and shoes were to be spit polished daily. His uniforms were so heavily starched that they would be at attention even when his body was at ease. Camaraderie was not a problem: Spike became close buddies with total strangers who had similarly cast their lot with the marines.

Spike accepted and met every challenge thrown his way during boot camp. With each conquest, no matter how slight, his self-confidence, self-esteem, and bearing were shaped and strengthened. He earned an Expert Rifle badge and set a new high score for individual performance on the demanding physical-readiness test. In making the most of the time allowed for personal hygiene, Spike learned to brush his teeth and shave while showering. He learned to run when he was weary. Spike studied his map reading, first aid, Marine Corps history, and infantry tactics assignments by flashlight under his blanket after the order for lights-out had been given.

No one knew or cared much about Spike's past. No one brought up his grades in school or berated him for not having earned his high-school diploma. As ironic as it may seem, it was Spike's first taste of life in Camelot. He was free at last. Not unlike the fictional character, Nora Helmer, in Henrik Ibsen's *A Doll's House*, Spike finally felt as if he was looked on as a real human being and was no longer shamed into behaving like an amiable nitwit.

The opportunity to be what he could be came to him only after escaping from a hometown where he was cast as a loser. Now he was liberated from arbitrary barriers to his personal development. Spike, who had never broken the law, was no longer labeled as delinquent. He was cut loose from the low expectations and lack of respect of his peers and teachers back home. At last, he was released from believing what he'd been told by everyone, except his mother: "Spike, just face the facts, man. You'll never amount to much in life!"

Over the next six months, Spike completed specialty training as a helicopter mechanic. Concurrently—and sparked by the kindness and encouragement of one of his instructors—Spike took advantage of the base education center, where he studied on weekends. One week before he completed his advanced training, Spike took the examination for his GED. The good news that he'd passed caught up with him about two months into his first tour of duty in the jungles of South Vietnam.

Lying in his hospital bed as his body healed and his mind cleared from the injuries sustained when his UH-1B helicopter (Huey) was shot down by ground fire, Spike decided to apply for Officer's Candidate School (OCS) at Quantico, Virginia. He'd have to reenlist for a few more years, but that was all right, because Spike had a fervid desire to return to the hot, humid jungles of Southeast Asia as an officer!

The ceremony was brief but dignified. "Spike" was no longer an appropriate moniker for Charles because it presented an image of him that had long since vanished into a repressed past filled with painful memories. Charles was now a first lieutenant. The rear admiral pinned the Navy Cross for heroism on the left pocket of the blouse of Charles's dress blues. The medal would take a position ahead of the Distinguished Flying Cross, Silver Star with oak leaf cluster, Bronze Star with V device, Purple Heart, and other campaign ribbons and service medals that already adorned his uniform.

Charles resigned his commission. His combined score of 1,460 on the SAT and his essay on the value of a higher education had earned him the opportunity to enroll as a freshman at a state college in southern California beginning the upcoming fall semester.

Graduating magna cum laude in engineering from college didn't hurt Charles's chances of signing on at Northrop. He wanted to live in the Los Angeles area where he could design fighter aircraft. He wanted to be partners with his lovely wife of four years in raising their children. He would help his mother find a place to live near them. His new job would allow him to help her financially.

On the one hand, "Spike" never did make it very big. On the other hand, he was a great help in building Charles's determination to realize his potential.

Charles still lives in the San Fernando Valley. He has yet to acquire a millionaire's fortune. His family has had its share of problems and dealt with them as well as they could. His mother lived nearby until she died. Charles never did design any new fighters, because his talent was for developing inertial guidance systems. In fact, he won several industry awards for his accomplishments in advanced missile technology.

Charles has never attended a high-school reunion, but more than one of his classmates has marveled in bewilderment over how Spike could ever have amounted to anything—he never earned one A!

Reflections on
Report Cards Get an F

The competitive instinct of the human creature is rarely satiated. We perpetually seek external confirmation of our individual ability, personal achievement, peer-group acceptance, and special importance. Report cards appeal to our competitive nature.

There has always been controversy over report cards and what the grades really mean. Report cards measure a student's performance against that of his or her classmates. Some people believe they predict future achievement. From time to time, enlightened teachers have graded student performance using criteria that measure individual progress—independent of classmates' performances.

Grades may be interpreted differently by administrators, teachers, parents and guardians, students, and siblings. Later in life, grades may assume significance for college admissions officers and for potential employers.

We are culturally obsessed with reports cards because we accept them as excellent universal referents by which all children can be judged. A flawed, if not simplistic, belief.

Reports cards are not inherently good or bad. They can objectively measure how well a student has progressed toward mastery of various subjects. They can provide information for students, teachers, administrators, and parents.

If, however, report cards measure individual students' performances against classmates' performances, they enhance neither teaching nor learning.

What grades tell is altogether too often who attended class, who handed in assignments, who wasn't disruptive, who wasn't tardy too often, whom the teacher liked, and how students compared academically with other students in the class.

What grades never tell you is whether or not the subject matter is useful to the student. Grades don't tell you if the student is bored. They don't tell you if the relationship between the teacher and the student or between the student and his or her peers is so bad that it interferes with learning. They don't tell you if the tests measured a true grasp of the subject or simply measured rote memory skill. They don't tell you if the student learned the material at home or at school. They never tell you if the student has mastered the subject matter, and they are defective indicators of future achievement.

Lessons Learned from Report Cards Get an F

Back in school, several of his classmates thought it funny, if not bizarre, that Spike couldn't even muster an A in physical education. Mr. Sanders, the boys physical education teacher, graded them on how fast they could run a mile, how far they could throw a softball, and so forth. He never graded them on whether or not they understood the rules of the sports they played or knew what the object of the sport was. Mr. Sanders graded on physical ability alone. Grading on the basis of hair and eye color would have been as meaningful in terms of true education.

• A student who earns straight A's gains the praise of his or her parents or guardians, a place on the school's honor role, the scorn of some of his or her peers, and you-make-me-look-stupid scowls from siblings with lower grades.

• Too often, a student with poor grades receives disapproval from parents and indifference from teachers. Unfortunately, the low regard of parents and teachers may extend to areas of the student's personality and ability that have nothing to do with academic performance.

• Suppose you were taking a course in parachuting and there were 100 things to learn to do successfully; you correctly identified 99 of these 100 items on the written test. But on your first jump, you couldn't remember how to pull the rip cord, which was the item you missed. You'd probably earn a posthumous A for the course from most teachers, but it wouldn't bring you back from the dead. If you want to jump safely, worry less about your test score and worry about what's important and what's not. Then learn and do the important things.

• There are a few teachers who establish objectives for their courses, then teach the content and provide opportunities for their students to practice and master each objective. At the end of the grading period, these teachers give a pass to everyone who has mastered the objectives and an incomplete to everyone who hasn't. What a lovely way to disrupt the system.

• If tardiness, absenteeism, and citizenship are important (and they are, because they have significant consequences), why not have a separate report card for them and not confuse them with academic achievement?

• Congratulations to those whose grades reflect dedication and diligent study in academically challenging courses. And to those who take hard courses that interest them although they risk lowering their grade average.

• Many times grades reflect a student's interest in the subject. Boredom may lead to low grades, involvement to high grades. But all achievers learn to override boredom, for they understand that not everything you encounter in school or on the job is interesting.

• The same student may earn straight A's in science and math, B's in physical education, and C's in music. Such is the nature of individual ability. We may each excel in some areas and not in others.

• The mediocre grades of unmotivated students don't reflect their true abilities. Their grades do, however, accurately measure their efforts. These students seem to be satisfied to be underachievers. No, they're not dumb, they just aren't motivated to do their best.

• Too often, report cards are used as weapons by teachers to control and reward students, by parents or guardians as the basis for criticism or praise by students to measure how they stacked up against peers, and by siblings to compare themselves to one another.

• What does ranking a student's academic performance against that of his or her peers have to do with anything? Maybe the competition was strong, maybe it was weak. What we ought to be interested in is whether or not students are fulfilling their own potential, what their interests are, and what deficiencies need to be corrected. Grades are poor measures of personal worth, can't measure individual potential, and never reliably predict future achievement.

• The brightest student is not always the one who can answer the most questions correctly. Rather, the brightest student may be the one who consistently identifies the wrong choices and avoids making them.

• Everyone ultimately loses when teachers and administrators train students to perform well on tests for the sole purpose of demonstrating that they, the educators, are doing an excellent job of educating and, therefore, deserve higher pay and better facilities. Competent administrators find other means of dealing with valid money issues.

• If the standards for individual performance are set low enough, mediocrity can earn straight A's or high marks on the job.

• Real education is not produced on an assembly line. Real education is a sloppy, well-intended process that involves teachers, administrators, parents or guardians, and students. Students need to develop social skills and healthy, positive attitudes about themselves and others. These aspects of a student's life cannot be measured by achievement tests or reflected on report cards.

• Although high grades and achievement test scores should not be an end unto themselves (nor can they define your level of personal achievement), they do have powerful effects on your life. Therefore, it is always best to earn the highest marks you can—and then press on.

11

The Phony Lure
of Fame and Fortune

Lucy Crane's *The Fisherman and His Wife* is a tale of insatiable greed that backfires.

As the story goes, one day a fisherman catches a large fish that talks. The fish asks the fisherman to let him go because he is really an enchanted prince. The fisherman complies with the request and returns home empty-handed telling his wife that although he has no fish, he did catch and release a large fish that was really an enchanted prince. His wife persuades the fisherman to return to the sea and ask the fish to grant him a wish in return for his kindness.

The fisherman asks the fish to grant his wife's wish, which is to turn their small hut into a little cottage. The fish tells the fisherman to return home; the wish has already been granted. But the wife soon tires of their little cottage and sends her husband back to the sea to ask the fish for a large stone castle. Reluctantly, the fisherman agrees and his wife's wish is granted.

Once again the wife becomes dissatisfied and asks for more. She gets her castle and becomes queen, then gets a palace and becomes empress. Yet again, the wife sends her husband back to the sea to ask the fish to make her ruler over the sun and the moon. The enchanted prince is finally fed up with the wife's greed and tells the fisherman to return home, where he will find his wife in their old hut.

Allen was a brilliant student. He did his undergraduate work at an Ivy League college and went on to earn an advanced degree in engineering.

He began his career in the aerospace industry, advancing rapidly and gaining wide acclaim as an engineer. Soon he was rejecting offers from rival companies for high-paying consulting work. Accepting these offers would have constituted a conflict of interest. They were, nevertheless, enticing.

Now Allen was a smart fellow, but he wasn't interested in relying on the uncertain income of "just another consultant." Before long, however, Allen was invited by a university to join its faculty. The dean promised him a light teaching load, ample opportunity to do research, clerical and editing support for papers and books he wrote, and, most important, several free days a month for outside consulting jobs.

The decision was an easy one. Allen accepted. Unlike the fisherman's wife, Allen worked hard for his rewards. And life was not just good, it was luxurious.

There was, however, a price to be paid. Allen was too busy teaching, writing, consulting, and entertaining clients to spend time with his wife and son. They all shared the same residence, but it wasn't a home. To his wife and son, Allen was a stranger who dropped by to sleep or to pick up fresh clothes before hitting the road again. Occasionally he did spend time with them, but his thoughts were elsewhere. Allen was not a bad man, but he was careless about his priorities. His neglect of his family was rooted in his insatiable lust for fame and fortune. Fame and fortune came. His wife and son went.

Stepping up to a professorship at a more prestigious university, Allen was soon making more money and enhancing his reputation further. There seemed to be no end in sight.

Allen's second wife was a woman who had a successful career, and wanted a husband who shared her ambitions. Whenever Allen and she found time for each other, they gloated over their past victories and planned new ones.

They lived a fairy tale of sheer happiness. After several years of increasing success, they had a son. Although they loved him very much, they didn't spend a lot of time with him. But he was never neglected, for his nanny delivered him to school, fed him, and rooted for him at his baseball games. Their son was not exceptionally bright, but he went to a fine private school where gifted teachers brought out the best in him.

Allen and his charming wife have traveled the world. They have dined with heads of state. Allen has published countless papers, delivered numerous addresses before large audiences, and written a dozen books. His second wife has been no less successful in her own right. They live in a beautiful, well-furnished home. They frequently entertain powerful and influential men and women. Both work very hard at their careers. They gained both fame and fortune. They are accomplished at everything they do, except at being available to their son. As a result, their son considers them failures as parents.

Several years have passed since their son graduated from college. They send him press clippings heralding their accomplishments and postcards showing the exotic places their assignments take them. When he visits them at "home," their son hears all about his father's and mother's latest triumphs. They don't seem interested in what he has been up to. They treat him like their other guests: Allen and his wife aren't genuinely interested in them either.

Reflections on
the Phony Lure of Fame and Fortune

Too often, in striving for more recognition and more money, people are guided by greed and vanity. They become addicted to acquisition. Longing for their next fix, they lose sight of decent values. As the fisherman's wife discovered, power and material possessions are ephemeral.

Concentrating exclusively on fame and fortune cost Allen the love of his first wife and son and his second son. While Allen and his second wife are not evil or dishonest, they are blind to the responsibilities and rewards of parenthood. On one hand, readers may believe that as parents, Allen and his wife have done just fine. They provided all that money can buy. Their son has never gone hungry or been left out in the cold. As a boy, he had his nanny for companionship and nurturing. On the other hand, readers may muse that the illustrious couple should have just gone out and bought a pet. But that's life, and, sadly enough, there are many sons and daughters who have been subjected to far greater parental neglect and abuse than Allen's son.

Most people aren't as greedy as the fisherman's wife. And the consequences of greedy, selfish behavior are not always immediately clear. But people who are attracted by the lure of fame and fortune are unaware of their weakness and its probable outcome. That is the nature of the lure.

Not all rich celebrities neglect their families and friends. Many of them are good people who contribute significantly to society. Perhaps, however, only a chosen few can keep affluence and media attention in perspective and control their appetites. In any case, as the tale of the fisherman's wife illustrates, if you aren't ever satisfied, no matter how rich and powerful you are, you may be reduced to humble circumstances.

Lessons Learned from
the Phony Lure of Fame and Fortune

It's surprising how many well-known, wealthy people honestly don't believe they have accomplished much. Conquering each new challenge has a way of silencing satisfaction and giving birth to new ambitions. Not surprisingly, few of the rich and famous knew at the outset how far they would go.

Most accomplished people never receive wide recognition. But does that make them any less successful? No! And that is the greatest lesson of all.

• If being the best and brightest student in your class is what you want, you may achieve it. But if you resort to earning this distinction at the expense of others, you'll have few friends and no one's respect.

• If you fall victim to the lure of fame and fortune, you don't have to stay in the trap. The road to recovery may be rocky, but you can travel it if you devote the same degree of passion to the journey that you devoted to achieving material success.

• You don't have to be rich or famous to neglect basic responsibilities to yourself and others.

• The normal desire to win the approval of others doesn't indicate that you're vain.

• Fortunes can be won through luck and lost through circumstance. But the battle for integrity is won or lost every day through your own efforts. The world needs men and women of integrity more than it needs rich and famous men and women.

• Greed and selfishness harm all their victims. You just hear more about the harm they do to the rich and famous.

• When others are too quick to flatter you or to give you credit for an accomplishment that wasn't yours, you are being manipulated.

• Genuine people don't live vain, fantasy-filled lives.

• The lure of fame and fortune is powerful and dangerous. It can make you do things you ought not do. So, should fame and fortune come your way, behave with humility and circumspection.

• The most important tributes that can be paid to you are the least likely to be newsworthy by today's standards.

• If you are solely motivated by a desire for money and media attention, you're being driven by the wrong passion, and although you may get rich and get notice, you may end up a sad disappointment to yourself.

12

Can You Believe
How Much Money He Makes?

"The Turnip" is a classic fable about jealousy and justice, greed and compassion, and sibling rivalry. It tells of two half-brothers who have little in common. The elder brother, a shrewd, pitiless man, believed personal wealth to be more important than compassion. A loan shark, in modern terms, he lived a life of ostentatious luxury while his half-brother led a meager life as a poor turnip farmer.

Everyone hated the rich half-brother. And no wonder! On the only occasion when the turnip farmer sought his help, he turned his dogs on his younger brother and shouted insults at him.

In contrast, the poor turnip farmer never turned a hungry person from his door. A man of paltry means, he willingly shared the best of what provisions he had, even with total strangers. One day an old cross-eyed man peered over the poor farmer's wall and asked him for a drink of water. The poor half-brother responded by giving him not only water, but also the best food he could find in his nearly bare pantry.

Several days later, the farmer's goodwill was rewarded when a great turnip appeared in his field. One thing led to another, and the turnip ended up before the king of the land. The king was impressed and asked about the character of the farmer. Finding him to be a good man, the king appointed him "the turnip provider in chief to the whole of the royal family." Soon the poor farmer was a wealthy man himself.

Unlike his rich half-brother, the now-wealthy turnip farmer shared all he had with the poor. Meanwhile, the elder half-brother was outraged because the farmer had achieved such prosperity from a turnip—a lowly form of produce indeed. Determined to upstage his half-brother, the rich man spent most of his fortune on the largest ruby in the land. He planned to give the ruby to the king. The king was so generous in his reward for one large turnip that surely the largest ruby in the land would fetch a fortune many times over. When the elder half-brother appeared in court, the king recognized him as a tightwad who indulged himself at the expense of the poor he robbed and the rich he cheated.

The king was less impressed by gifts than by the giver. He admired character. Accepting the ruby, the king told the rich man that he would send a reward to him—something the king valued beyond words. Throughout the night, the rich man waited in eager anticipation of the reward that would arrive the next day. The next morning, the royal party reached his home in full regalia. The king's servants pulled back the canvas that covered the wagon. Stunned and dismayed by what the king had sent as his reward for the largest ruby in the land, the rich man ran away, as far and as fast as his porcine body would allow before he dropped to his death. There in the wagon, on a large dish, lay the king's gift: a slice of the giant turnip given him by the rich man's half-brother. Motivated all his life by the love of money, the rich man couldn't endure receiving a just reward.

Ray shook his boss's hand and thanked her for understanding his shocking decision. After some twenty-five years with one of the world's largest manufacturing firms, Ray was walking away from a decent salary—by industry standards—a secure future with the company, and a healthy number of stock options that would be exercisable over the next few years. He owned a lovely home in one of the more desirable areas of the community. Ray and his family had developed a circle of close friends in the company, at their church, and in the community at large. After all his years of hard work to get to where he was, how could he accept a position in a less desirable city, in a smaller and less prestigious company?

Over the years Ray had proven himself a good company man. He had been willing to uproot his family and move to any location management chose. A team player, Ray had accepted some of those high-risk, low-payoff, thankless job assignments found in every big organization. He expected more rewarding positions in later years and was willing to pay the price. Ray had never displayed the mental agility, bureaucratic acumen, or killer instinct of the chosen few on the corporate fast track. He was a plodder, a decent sort of guy who would never stab a fellow worker in the back. He was extraordinarily patient as a manager and overly tolerant of weaknesses in his subordinates. Ray was honest in all his dealings and gave people at work and in his personal life the benefit of the doubt.

After twenty years with the company, he was finally promoted to senior management. And that's where his disillusionment began.

As a senior executive, Ray's job performance and management instincts came under fire. He was told that formerly minor faults in his style were now major flaws. He would never be head of the division unless he corrected them.

He tried to improve his performance, but one of his subordinates was promoted over him and was now head of the division and his boss. Ray believed he had taught her everything she knew about the business but not everything he knew about it. He became disenchanted with the company.

Then a new chairman joined the firm. Cost-cutting measures were introduced to help his company compete with foreign and domestic companies that suddenly challenged them in markets they once dominated. The executive dining room was closed. First-class air travel for company executives was withdrawn. Reserved parking spaces and company-paid memberships in a country club were done away with. Gone in a flash were the amenities for which he had worked so hard and waited so long. To Ray executive perks were important. He boasted of them to his friends and neighbors; they represented recognition won on the battlefield of corporate America. The grim reaper had struck: There would be no turning back to a more sybaritic lifestyle. Ray decided to break his ties with the only company he had ever worked for.

One of Ray's former colleagues was now the president of a smaller, rival firm. The firm's senior management was recruiting experienced senior executives. Ray qualified and signed on with a considerable raise in pay; the perks taken away by his previous employer were part of the package at the new firm.

Thrilled at the prospect of becoming an executive vice-president, Ray resigned from his old job. His boss listened in amazement as Ray described his new package of benefits and perks. She couldn't understand how anyone could think that Ray was worth so much. Several days later, after Ray's new job had become the focus of office gossip, his colleagues didn't speak of his years of service to the company nor of the frequent moves he and his family had made. Instead they kept repeating, "Can you believe how much money he makes?"

*Reflections on Can You Believe
How Much Money He Makes?*

Fascination with the personal wealth and financial good fortune of other people afflicts rich and poor alike.

Newspapers rank professional athletes according to their relative earnings. *Forbes* magazine annually lists the wealthiest people in America. *Business Week* publishes an issue every year on executive compensation. What's the point? Does how much the senior executives make influence whether or not we buy their company's stock? Does it influence whether or not we do business with their company? Should we weep and wail because we aren't as rich as the richest? Does their yearly compensation indicate that we are grossly underpaid? The reality is, that's what they were paid and someone approved it. And when they're no longer considered worth big money, they'll earn less—maybe nothing. That's how it works for professional athletes and professional executives alike.

We are also told by the media how underpaid or overpaid elected officials are in comparison with managers in private enterprise. And we know that teachers in our public schools are shamefully underpaid, but because raising their pay involves raising taxes, many taxpayers resist supporting our schools.

No objective answer exists to the question: How much is she (or he) worth? But consider another question: So what does it mean to you? If other people get paid more than you, are you a less-worthy person? Can you justify a raise in your own pay based on what other people make? Is money the most important thing?

In both "The Turnip" and the vignette about Ray, we find a common thread: If you work hard, stay on track, and share your talents with others, you will be rewarded.

Lessons Learned from Can You Believe How Much Money He Makes?

The reward for doing your best in school may not be straight A's or even one A. Your reward for doing your best on the job may not be a promotion and big money and perks. But in both cases you will be rewarded by the respect of others, you'll probably have lots of friends, and you'll have your personal dignity—something that money doesn't buy.

If you concentrate on your own work, help others, and don't worry about what they get on their report cards or in their paychecks, you'll be a lot happier than if you become bitter and envious.

The following insights put your relationships with grades and money into perspective:

• There is nothing wrong with getting good grades. Furthermore, class rankings on the basis of merit are useful. But those who are jealous of the marks other people earn are doomed to disappointment.

• Most of us have ample opportunity to succeed regardless of what is on our report cards, as long as we do our best.

• An irony inherent in our school systems is that some students strive to become educated and get good grades in the process, while other students strive only to get good grades and become educated in the process.

• Jealousy is demeaning. Avoid it and strive to be your best self. If you are out of touch with your best self, have the courage to change. You'd be surprised how many people would be willing to help you improve yourself. You need only to ask.

• The measure of personal achievement is different for everyone. And so it follows that one person's idea of success may not hold true for another. For example some people strive to make lots of money, others find joy in being creative forces in the arts, and still others devote themselves to their families and communities.

• There is no shame in amassing wealth through honest competition in the marketplace. Conversely, there is no shame in not amassing wealth through honest competition in the marketplace.

• When you try to earn high marks by conning your teachers, you may end up with an appropriate reward—but it may not please you.

• If you are jealous of someone else's money or in awe of the rich, you are focusing on unimportant aspects of life. What is important is to earn enough to meet your own needs, to use what you have wisely, and to respect men and women who achieve whatever they have through dignified means. In their case, the means really do justify the end.

• Rich people aren't necessarily wretched. In fact, rich people who give generously to worthy people and causes can be good company.

• Financial success contains no guarantee against financial failure. So a sense of personal achievement must not depend only on how much money you make.

• Without competition, businesses slow down. But with competition, far too many business leaders feel compelled to win at any cost. And when they do win, the gain is only short lived. In the long run, they and lots of other people lose.

• Last, keep in mind that someone else's good grades or financial success does not diminish your own achievements. In other words, the tree of jealousy bears bitter fruit.

13

The Pitfall of False Pride

Narcissus, a romantic character in Greek mythology, was an astonishingly beautiful man. So enticing was Narcissus's physical beauty that he attracted the love and affection of males and females alike. His false pride led him to spurn them all.

According to myth, the young man was under the care of the virgin-huntress and twin sister of Apollo, Artemis, a goddess of the chase and of wood nymphs. Artemis didn't want anyone to abuse those in her care. So when Echo, a wood nymph, pleaded with Narcissus to love her, and Narcissus rejected her, Artemis made him fall in love with himself as punishment.

Tragedy followed. After hours of sitting on the edge of a pond where he gazed passionately at the reflection of his own beauty, Narcissus was so overcome by his self-love that he killed himself. Artemis had made him the victim of his own beauty.

• • •

James was born into a family of possession and priv-
ilege. He attended private boarding schools with boys
from similar backgrounds. Living apart from his family, he suffered periods of loneliness and felt aban-
doned from time to time, but James was being
groomed to take his place among the titans of business
and industry.

Many of his prep school friendships continued
through his years at an Ivy League college. Perhaps
out of guilt James's parents showered him with love
and affection during breaks from school. A few months
before earning his master of business administration
(MBA) degree, James was introduced by his father to
a legend of Wall Street who was intrigued by this
young gentleman's demeanor and wit.

James began his career as an assistant to this legendary figure. Through the exposure his first job af-
forded him, James's learning curve was accelerated,
and he was soon dazzling men many years his senior.
Moving through the ranks of management with ease,
James was heralded by several prominent business
journals as one of the bright stars in corporate America. Not to anyone's great surprise, at a very young
age, he became the chief executive officer of one of
Wall Street's most respected brokerage firms. He had
always earned straight A's in school and was now bat-
ting 1.000 in the major leagues of business. He never
even dirtied his uniform—made from the finest Italian
silks and accessorized with diamonds and gold, status
symbols of success.

James soon became the subject of numerous business articles. His photograph adorned the cover of prestigious journals. He was profiled over and over again—a role model for others who wanted a fast ride to the top at a young age. His college honored him as a distinguished alumnus. He was a frequent and popular speaker at business schools. His future seemed boundless.

What the public recognized, but James never understood, was that many doors had been opened by the old-boy network of family contacts. Many of the obstacles encountered by less well-connected executives had been removed for James. When he fought on the corporate battlefield, his weapons were superior to those of many of his opponents. Furthermore, James's mentors shielded him. He was not required to make independent decisions and was not always held accountable for his disasters.

His rise to the top was swift; he was popular among his peers and with his subordinates. Soon James began to believe in his own infallibility. He no longer required the advice and counsel of mentors, peers, or subordinates. He could do better by himself. Suggestions and recommendations from his staff met with heavy faultfinding. Warning and counsel from mentors of the past were ignored. Most alarming of all was his failure to keep up his contacts in the old-boy network. His former friends, who were now in positions of power at rival firms, no longer had a place in his life. After all, they just wanted a piece of his action, and he wasn't about to make it easy for them.

It takes hard work to screw up a good thing. James, through a combination of making irrational business decisions and alienating everyone he came in contact with, began to screw up a healthy business. The press, formerly generous, now questioned his competence. Company finances rapidly eroded. Several key executives joined competing firms and took many of their major accounts with them. Although he considered himself bulletproof, James's imminent fall from glory grew close. The press turned on him viciously. The board of directors lost confidence in him. The once bright star of Wall Street had imploded. James, like the mythical Narcissus, had fallen victim to his own false pride.

Reflections on
the Pitfall of False Pride

Had Narcissus, the legendary character in Greek mythology, used his natural beauty and talents modestly and judiciously, he might have been included among the romantic heroes.

Similarly, if James, a talented and bright business star, had continued to rely on other people as well as on himself, he would probably be heading up a successful corporation today. These two appealing figures let their pride lead to their graceless undoing.

There is nothing wrong with being proud of your abilities and accomplishments. There is, however, something very wrong with believing in your superiority over others and with believing that you are invincible and others have nothing to offer you. It is a pitfall—the pitfall of false pride.

Lessons Learned from the Pitfall of False Pride

James's story is unusual, but not rare. Even privileged men and women who have been groomed for years to occupy senior leadership positions can fall victim to their own false pride. If it can happen to them, it can certainly happen to those who must make it to the top more or less on their own.

Pride is a powerful motivation. Personal pride can enable one to reach one's goals. People who take pride in their work perform better than those who don't—at school and at work.

There is danger, however, in excessive pride. When you begin to believe that you are solely responsible for your own success, trouble begins. You believe you are smarter than anyone else; no one else is quite up to your standards; you believe you no longer require other people's support to achieve your goals; you just know you can meet and conquer any challenge alone. And the most telling point of all is that false pride infects people in all walks of life and at every level of an organization. The results are never good.

There are some principles worth noting on the pitfall of false pride. They can help you avoid falling victim to your own best attributes:

• Taking pride in your schoolwork and in learning pays big dividends in terms of grades, recognition, self-confidence, and accomplishment.

• Taking pride in your work pays big dividends in terms of compensation, promotions, and relations with your boss and co-workers.

• As strange as it may seem, some of the smartest students and brightest people on the job are unfulfilled and abnormal. There is more to success and happiness than simply acquiring skills and knowledge.

• You don't earn natural physical beauty, you inherit it. Be grateful for your physical advantages and keep up your personal appearance. But remember that success is not found in being just another pretty face.

• People whose achievements attract the attention of the media find both their virtues and their weaknesses exaggerated by reporters. So, if you are noticed by the media, don't take it to heart. Reports won't be entirely accurate nor will they ensure your future success or failure—unless you let them.

• Achievement in school or on the job is not gained through your solo efforts. You rely on teachers, friends, and family to help you do your best in school. You rely on bosses, co-workers, customers, family, and friends to help you excel at your job. If you ever begin to think you don't need help—you're in the danger zone.

• You become vulnerable to failure at the moment you begin to believe you're infallible.

• Be proud of your personal appearance and your accomplishments. But avoid the resentment of others— even gain their respect—by not flaunting your looks or achievements.

14

Pygmalion and Performance Appraisals

Pygmalion was a sculptor and a king of Cyprus. He hated women until, according to Greek legend, he fell in love with one of his own creations, an ivory statue of Aphrodite—the Greek goddess of erotic love and marriage. Pygmalion then prayed for his statue to come to life. His prayers were answered, and he married the goddess, Aphrodite. This legend of Pygmalion has been told and retold, with variations on the theme.

In Sir William S. Gilbert's "Pygmalion and Galatea," the sculptor is a married man. The comedy is based partly on the legend of Pygmalion and partly on the classical legend of Acis. In Acis, a handsome young Sicilian shepherd loves the sea nymph Galatea. He loses his life in combat with a jealous rival, the Cyclops Polyphemus. In Gilbert's comedy, the character of the sculptor is based on Pygmalion. The sculptor's wife, Cynisca, becomes jealous of his relationship with his newly animated statue of Galatea, and Galatea is transformed back into her original form as a lifeless statue.

In George Bernard Shaw's twentieth-century play, "Pygmalion," Professor Henry Higgins transforms a Cockney flower girl Eliza Doolittle from a street urchin into an elegant and sophisticated woman. Although Eliza falls in love with the professor, she doesn't marry him. Because she no longer looks or acts like a flower girl, the professor finds her a more appropriate job.

In psychological terms, *Pygmalionism* describes a condition characterized by falling in love with one's own creation. In the world of education, the *Pygmalion effect* describes an unexpected improvement in student performance that is attributed to teachers' high expectations of students (based on the teachers' belief that high test scores are real when they are artificially inflated). The explanation may be that the teachers become more involved with these students and encourage them more than their previous teachers have. The affected students are, as a result, motivated to perform at a higher level than they have in the past.

Whenever it is used, the term Pygmalion implies we behave according to the expectations of influential people around us.

A task force of corporate human resources managers had been quickly organized to study the unexpected increase in lawsuits filed against one of the subsidiary companies. A small unit, the subsidiary had a low overhead and was highly profitable. Providing an essential mail-order fulfillment service for another subsidiary company, the operation was an integral component of the corporation. Even more important than the number of lawsuits was the threat of union activity at the subsidiary. It was a situation requiring immediate action.

After two weeks of study, the corporate task force presented their action plan to the president of the subsidiary's division. The action plan called for bold steps, because the situation was close to being beyond resolution. A union vote was expected soon, perhaps before the lawsuits could be settled. The task force also reported that the subsidiary's human resources manager wasn't capable of handling this high-risk situation.

You'd think that a young Turk on the corporate staff would be eager to take charge of the troubled subsidiary. All he'd have to do is minimize the financial damage from the lawsuits and keep the company union free. If he could accomplish that, he'd be a corporate hero. But every member of the task force considered the downside risk too great. So when the president asked who should be assigned the job of "fixing the inauspicious situation," no one volunteered.

Ah, but they had a recommendation. Wade was just the person for the task. He was new to the company so he didn't know enough to turn the assignment down. He was the human-resources director in a unit of the company that was running very well. And Wade had seasoned subordinates to keep things in line during his absence. Moreover, he had a reputation for taking high risks and had already solved a few very tough employee-relations problems in his short tenure with the company. Wade was anxious to prove himself capable of broader assignments. If he really wanted the chance to show his stuff, this was the opportunity.

You guessed it—the smooth-talking division president called Wade in and briefed him on the situation. "You should be pleased to learn that your human-resources colleagues think you are the only person in the company that can settle the lawsuits and resolve the employee-relations problems in this unit," he told Wade. "I've called the new president we've placed in charge of the operation. He is expecting you tomorrow. I know you'll get the job done. Let's talk in a week and discuss your plan."

Wade thought, "Here is a situation so bad that not one of the corporate staff studying the situation is willing to risk his or her reputation on it. They know the problems, they know the management team, they know the unit's human-resources manager; yet they have nominated me? This is trouble, but if they don't have the guts to fix it, all I can do is fail. And, that's really what they expect to happen."

Wade accepted the assignment. He never read the task force's report, but he took some very nervy steps. Meeting the problems head-on, he completed the assignment in five weeks—a full three months ahead of the task force's most optimistic estimate. Wade required very little company money to settle the lawsuits. He provided the unit's new management team with basic training in human relations that enabled them to keep the union out. And not much more was required. The problem had been misunderstood and greatly exaggerated by the task force.

Wade earned high marks for his performance under extraordinary circumstances. He was now a combat veteran, a major problem solver, a risk taker. He proved that he was at his best in the heat of battle.

Soon another employee-relations monster raised its ugly head in another division. Dangerous duty once again called, and Wade was drafted.

This new assignment required relocation for Wade and his family. The problem took three long years of grueling effort on his part to resolve. Along the way he was wounded a few times, but not fatally so. He survived until the unit in jeopardy was running smoothly. Then Wade was no longer needed. His performance appraisals described him as a problem solver, a firefighter. But as soon as there were no more corporate fires to put out, Wade became a victim of corporate typecasting. The corporation that had cast him in the role of firefighter discarded him when there were no more fires to put out.

Reflections on Pygmalion and Performance Appraisals

Wade wasn't naive. He performed best when the stakes were high. He recognized that success with the first dangerous assignment could earn him a label as a troubleshooter, perhaps even a loose cannon, within the organization. But he wasn't concerned with his future in the organization. He could always find another job. And he did. Odd as it seemed to his former colleagues, his new job didn't involve organizational troubleshooting. Wade's story is an everyday example of Pygmalion and performance appraisals. And the phenomenon holds true for the classroom too.

If you have a history of being disruptive in the classroom, your teachers will expect you to be disruptive and call you down for even a slight disruption, while more disruptive peers with no reputations as troublemakers can act up without being criticized. And straight C students can really have a tough time bringing up their grades when their teachers don't encourage them as much as they do students with better grades. Yet teachers who are Pygmalions in the classroom are behaving quite naturally. Most bosses and teachers are influenced by how they feel about a subordinate or a student.

At one time or another, we can all play both Pygmalion—the creator who strongly molds another—and the object of a Pygmalion. Conversely what others think about us and how they treat us does affect us. How we behave toward others has consequences for them and for us. These effects are consequences either positive or negative, but never neutral.

The day you get your report card in school, or your performance appraisal at work, is usually stressful. Why? Because your worth as a student or as an employee is being evaluated. Because you are being ranked against your classmates or your peers. Because no evaluation is completely objective, nor are you likely to be certain before you receive your evaluation of how you stand in the eyes of your teacher or your boss. And what your teacher or your boss thinks of you influences your opportunities for success.

In one sense, it really doesn't matter how you're evaluated. If you've done your best, you are a person of integrity. And neither report cards nor performance appraisals can strip you of your integrity. Nevertheless, you have to live with the more immediate consequences of your report cards and performance appraisals, good or bad. So it is in your own best interest to get the highest evaluations you can while maintaining your integrity.

Lessons Learned from Pygmalion and Performance Appraisals

There are many good things to be gained from respectable grades and from high performance appraisals. And although you can't usually control all the variables that go into your evaluations at school or work, you can influence both of them a great deal. To that end, here are a few lessons you may find useful:

• Getting better grades than your peers doesn't mean you're a superior person. It just means you're successful in school. And don't be surprised later to find yourself working for an average student who has become successful in business.

• If you want your teachers to think highly of you, attend class, do your homework, and contribute to classroom discussion.

• Pygmalion's error wasn't in creating a work of art or in bringing it to life, it was in attempting to possess Aphrodite after she received life. Possessive teachers and bosses need to learn to let go of the people they help to form.

• If students are told they are too dumb, stupid, or lazy to learn, they'll probably fulfill those low expectations.

• If you have a reputation at work that you don't like, and have tried to shake it off, consider finding a new job and building a new reputation.

• At school and on the job, it is easier to establish a positive reputation than to overcome a soiled one.

• Tailor your behavior to suit the reputation you desire.

• Subordinates usually perform well if the boss expects them to succeed.

• If you want your boss to value you as an employee, begin by showing up. Then do your job to the best of your ability. And if you have spare time, ask how else you can be useful.

• You may at some point receive a report card or a performance appraisal that you believe to be unfair. You won't be alone; most people have this experience. You can, however, grade or assess others fairly. Praise them for what they accomplish and encourage them to improve in areas of weakness.

• There is no guarantee that you'll receive a great report card or performance appraisal even if you've done your best. But when you have done your best, don't lose your personal dignity no matter how your teachers or bosses evaluate you.

• If your boss constantly expects you to behave in a way you find disagreeable, it's time to find a new boss. In doing so, you'll retain your dignity and self-respect, both of which are more easily lost than restored.

• Sometimes you pay a high price for being true to yourself. The decision is often a difficult one, but it is always yours to make and should be made with integrity.

• And last, it is more important to think well of yourself than to have others think well of you. Furthermore, whatever you do to feel good about yourself can also elicit approval from others. But bear in mind that what others think of you does matter to some degree, even if you're right and they're wrong. We have a name for people who are completely indifferent to what other people think of them: It's *psychopath*, but then again, it may also be *artist*. Van Gogh, for instance, didn't change his style to please others. Now there's a gorgeous museum devoted only to his work. He suffered and did not live to enjoy the fame and fortune his paintings elicit. But he was right about his art and his contemporaries were wrong. He acted, as you should be advised, with integrity.

15

Bullies Don't Have
Happy Birthday Parties

One day a wizard paid a visit to the king of a rich and vast land. The wizard had seen in a vision that the king would die in five years and felt compelled to inform him. The wizard's message dismayed the king, but he decided to use his remaining time by planning and implementing an orderly succession to his throne. It was a duty that would require careful consideration as succession to the throne by the oldest prince or princess had been abolished by his own father's decree. Now, the most capable prince was to be named successor to the king.

The king had twin sons, Prince Hector and Prince Zachary. They had been educated by the best and wisest tutors in the kingdom and had mastered all the subjects taught to them. Neither seemed to have any physical advantage over the other; they were both strong and powerful. Each had recently married a fine young woman from a royal family in a neighboring kingdom. Having sons with so much in common would make choosing the one best suited to become his heir a formidable task for the king.

On the twin princes' next birthday, the king gave a party in their honor. During the afternoon, he met privately with his sons and told them of the wizard's vision. The young princes were saddened by the news of the father's approaching death but happy that they would have him with them for five more years.

The king then told them that he must decide which of them was best suited to ascend the throne. So he had devised a plan. He would give each of them stewardship over a small portion of his kingdom. In four years, they would meet again, and the princes would report on what they had accomplished in their provinces. The one who had performed his duties best would be the next king.

Prince Hector and his bride rode in a great carriage to their new castle on the edge of a beautiful, winding river. After giving the servants instructions on how to honor him and demanding a more exquisite menu for the royal household, he called together all the farm overseers in his province. Prince Hector announced that he was setting higher standards of production for the farms. Meeting them would require longer workdays, but the stakes were high—he was determined to become the new king.

When the overseers left, Prince Hector called for the royal thespians; he wanted to be entertained. Then he sent for the royal huntsman; he wanted to bag game from his new forest. Meanwhile, the overseers had returned to their farms and had told all the farmhands about their increased production quotas and longer workdays.

Prince Zachary and his bride rode on horseback to their new castle, which was pleasantly situated in a grove of trees at the base of a high mountain. As they rode, they paused to speak to a number of the farmhands in their new province. Shortly after arriving at their castle, the prince and princess met with their servants and asked them about the routines and menu that had been established for the royal family they were replacing. Thanking them for the information, the prince told them they were not to change anything for two weeks. During that period, the staff was to consider any changes they would like him to make to improve their efficiency or to lighten their burdens so they could spend more time with their own families. He would meet with them again in a fortnight.

Prince Zachary then invited his overseers to meet him at the edge of a lake near his castle for a feast. As the feast was drawing to a close, the prince told the overseers he planned to visit each of their farms. He would not only meet their farmhands and their families but he would also inspect their livestock and fields. In preparation for his visit, the overseers and their farmhands were to make a list of improvements they needed for their farms. Prince Zachary would consider their ideas seriously. Then he and his bride rode up onto the mountain by themselves. There they continued their honeymoon while all who were now under their care considered the assignments the prince had given them.

Four years passed and the princes returned to their father's castle to celebrate their birthday and to report to the king on their stewardship over the provinces he had granted them.

Prince Hector was pleased to inform his father and brother that production had improved so much in his province that he had increased its annual contribution to the kingdom's treasury by 30 percent each year. The king asked Prince Hector what he had done to achieve such amazing growth. Prince Hector told how he'd increased workdays and reduced holidays, how he'd taken all children over ten years old out of school so they could help their parents with the crops and livestock, and how he'd cut back on the share each farm received of what it produced.

The king then asked Prince Hector if the people in his province were happy under his rule. The prince told his father that his people were like royal subjects everywhere—always complaining, frequently and habitually incompetent. The king asked his son how he'd spent his own time during his brief reign. Prince Hector told his servants to fetch and display his trophies for the king. "Father, I have become a great hunter," Prince Hector proudly replied.

Then it was Prince Zachary's turn to account for his stewardship. "And what have you accomplished, my son?" the king asked.

"Father, I'm afraid I haven't increased my province's contribution to your treasury as dramatically as has my brother," he said. Then Prince Zachary told how he had discovered that the people in his province were treated badly by their former ruler and how he'd provided them with new plows, helped them mend the harnesses for their workhorses, and organized craftsmen to patch leaky roofs. The prince said he'd cut down the waste of valuable foodstuffs in the royal castle by eating from less elegant menus and eliminating the frequent ostentatious feasts his predecessor held. Prince Zachary went on to relate that he'd instructed his overseers to tend the fields and flocks. Much to his brother's surprise, Prince Zachary said that his increase to the treasury of his father's kingdom could have been greater, but he'd built new schools for the children in his province. And there was one more factor that affected the financial return of his province. Prince Zachary had increased the share of the farm profits granted to his overseers and their farmhands.

The king then asked his son if the people were happy with his rule. "I think so, Father," he said. "They always seem to be cheerful in their work, there is little sickness, and I'm impressed by how well they perform every task and go out of their way to help one another."

"And how have you been spending your own time, my son?" the king inquired.

"Oh, I have started my own garden in the backyard of the castle. I raise some of my own food, so the servants can spend more time with their families," Prince Zachary said. "I also keep animals in a shed near the castle." And then he went on to tell the king about how he'd been teaching in the schools from time to time, and how he frequently visited the families in his land.

"Haven't you been doing any hunting or fishing?" the king asked.

"Well, I like hunting and fishing," Prince Zachary

said. "But there has been so much to do that I haven't had time. Next month, if nothing interferes, I do plan a few days in the woods with my princess."

Then the king announced to those gathered at his sons' birthday party that he'd reached a decision about which of his two fine sons would be the new king. For Prince Zachary it was a great birthday party. No one is sure where Prince Hector went after the king's announcement, but it is generally believed that he went hunting.

She doesn't look like a bully. But the reserved, well-mannered, and conservatively dressed Lisa is one of the biggest bullies in the company. Underneath the fine silk and linen and the counterfeit charm is a raging monster.

Lisa is from a family with strong traditional values. Her father was a good and responsible man who always had time for his wife and children. He was a plumber who sent his three children to a private elementary school and to a respected university in Pennsylvania. Her mother had a part-time job in a local supermarket and sent her children to summer camp in the nearby mountains. Lisa's family attended religious services each Sunday. None of the children caused problems in or out of school. Unlike her brother and sister, who ran around with a bunch of other children, Lisa had only one or two friends.

After graduation from college, Lisa landed her first job—on the strength of her grades. She attacked her assignments with vigor and a determination to get ahead quickly. Whatever was asked of her, she did—usually alone. She wanted all the credit for herself. On the rare occasions when an assignment was late or incomplete, she always blamed someone else for failing to provide her with information or support.

In companies experiencing rapid growth, as Lisa's was, the wrong person is often selected to fill an open management slot. Lisa is a case in point. Although she was not a leader and frequently alienated people, she was available for an entry-level manager's position that opened up. Her management thought she could get the job done although her skill with people was marginal. They hoped Lisa would develop her management abilities.

Lisa accepted the job, and from her first day as a new supervisor, she jumped all over her staff, demanding that they improve. Her staff wasn't convinced she knew the first thing about her new job and cooperated reluctantly.

Although Lisa was able to complete most of the reports and projects assigned to her unit over the next six months, she blamed ones that slipped through the cracks on staff turnover, staff absences, and incompetence in people she had inherited with the job.

About a year into the job, Lisa's management realized that she was cooperative with them and talked a good line, but she couldn't be counted on to carry the responsibilities inherent in her position.

Her manager talked to Lisa about her inability to get things done and the low morale in her unit. As in the past, Lisa denied her failures and rattled off a list of her past accomplishments. Her boss reminded Lisa that her past accomplishments weren't in question. The focus was on her past failures. Outraged, Lisa demanded that she be allowed to speak to her boss's boss.

Lisa did gain an audience with her boss's boss, but the outcome was hardly what she expected. He listened carefully to her side of the story and then compared it to what he knew of her past performance. He warned her that he, too, was concerned about her inability to manage her unit, her refusal to accept criticism, and her habit of blaming others for her own failures. To make matters worse, no one liked working in her unit. Lisa was going to have to change.

Lisa did change—jobs. She denied responsibility for her actions and blamed her problems on ineffective managers who didn't understand high performers.

Reflections on
Bullies Don't Have Big Birthday Parties

Bullies are often portrayed as underprivileged, sinister, and sneaky. Prince Hector was none of these. He was privileged and felt he didn't have to earn respect—he could demand it. His brother, Prince Zachary, realized that he had to win the hearts and minds of his people. Pushing them around and taking away their limited privileges was no way to gain a strong following.

The nature of organizations and the shortage of qualified candidates for entry-level jobs worked to Lisa's advantage. She is now working pushing people around in a different company. It's a cycle that is likely to be repeated every twelve to eighteen months or until Lisa realizes she needs to change her behavior if she wants to become a successful manager.

Lessons Learned from
Bullies Don't Have Big Birthday Parties

Bullies don't always look mean, and they are not necessarily male. They may be rich or poor, well educated or poorly educated. They may be found almost anywhere.

Keep in mind that you don't have to be a boss to abuse other people. You can threaten and intimidate without ever being in charge.

Here are some important lessons about bullies that will help you deal more effectively with them and perhaps keep you from becoming one yourself:

• At school, a bully tries to gain approval and attention by irresponsible manipulation of classmates.

• Bullies may not be driven out of schools or organizations, but they'll be avoided even by their teachers and bosses. It is hard to achieve much on the job or in school without the help of teachers and bosses.

• Toadies are a bully's only cronies. They are usually so easily swayed, and their loyalty is so shallow, that they can't be counted on in tough times. But then no bully deserves loyalty.

• Bullies thrive on confrontations. They always have to be right and in control. And they are quick to run to their toadies for consolation and reassurance.

• At work, the bully attempts to achieve recognition by manipulating the boss, demeaning peers, intimidating subordinates, and denying all responsibility for their own antisocial behavior.

• Bullies are cowards and usually pick on people below them in the organization. But once in a while a bully gets reckless and picks on the boss. This is a quick way for a bully to become the victim.

• Everybody has personality flaws. A bully's personality flaws are always in evidence, and that makes him or her hard to deal with on a daily basis.

• When given a choice, people reject a bully. You need support from other people to be successful, and bullies don't get it.

• Bullies habitually coerce, threaten, and browbeat others. Yet they are unaware they do these things automatically.

• When you bully your subordinates, you gain only minimal support.

• High-achieving bullies lead double lives. They suck up to the boss and abuse subordinates.

• And in conclusion, remember that bullies will do almost anything to escape the consequences of their behavior. When they feel threatened, they'll even betray their toadies.

16

Chasing Windmills Only Makes You Tired

Miguel de Cervantes's *Don Quixote de la Mancha* is a seventeenth-century novel. The protagonist is Alonso Quixano, an obliging, gracious, and simpleminded country gentleman who changes his name to Don Quixote. Mocked in a materialistic world, Quixano reads too many romances of chivalry and loses touch with reality. The book tells of his adventures when he thinks he is Don Quixote.

"Knighted" by an innkeeper whose wretched roadhouse he mistakes for a castle, Quixote rides away on a bony old nag; he is going into the world to avenge all wrongs. During his travels, Don Quixote imagines, among other things, that the windmills he passes are giants he must slay. He tilts his lance at one too many windmills—to no avail—and experiences a variety of other setbacks. A weary and disenchanted Quixote returns to his home where, shortly before his death, he renounces books that tell tales of wandering knights.

Despondent, Merrill sat at his desk holding his head in his hands. How was he going to tell his wife and children that he had been fired from his high-profile, executive position that August afternoon. With two children in college and a mortgage on his house, he knew his token severance payment and meager savings wouldn't last long.

Merrill was neither uneducated nor unemployable. He had a doctorate in educational administration. He had started his career teaching in a good public high school. His rise to the principalship had been swift. Over the ten years of his tenure, student academic performance had steadily improved; the school sent some fine athletes on to good universities, too. In fact, 80 percent of his high school's graduates went to college. Teachers' contract negotiations were resolved without strikes or boycotts. Parent volunteerism increased significantly; the parent-teacher association was active.

Merrill was, by every measure, one of the best principals that a student or parent could hope for. But Merrill's success bred boredom. The challenges of his position had been met, and he was restless. He began to inquire about new job opportunities.

Two positions were immediately offered to Merrill. One was as a senior administrator with the state department of education; the other was as an associate professor at a major university. Seeking advice from a businessman he knew, about which job to take, Merrill was presented with an unexpected and exciting opportunity. The businessman had just been hired by a closely held family corporation to head up a major commercial real estate project. This was a new project to be undertaken locally, and the owners were hiring local executives to manage it.

Never before had Merrill considered a career in business. He wasn't confident that he had the skills for an executive position in commercial real estate development. "Don't worry. I'll teach you all you need to know about commercial real estate and project management," the businessman had told him. "Besides, your two children will soon be off to college, and the jobs you've been offered in education pay a pauper's salary compared to what you'll make with me. Sign on, and your kids will never have to worry about college expenses. You've been extraordinarily successful as a school principal, and managing in business isn't any different from managing a high school."

Merrill should have known better, but the promise of a high salary, a bonus opportunity, and exciting perks enticed him into making a hasty decision to join the well-financed new company in a position for which he was not qualified.

All of Merrill's initial expectations were then met. He had access to leaders in the business community as well as to government officials who were enthusiastic about this new development. Merrill and his wife went to up-scale social gatherings. The company paid for their season tickets to the symphony, ballet, and opera, which they attended with great pleasure. Frequently, they used the company's tickets to attend professional and college sporting events, too. The company provided him with a luxury sedan and membership at a country club. Life couldn't get any better, as far as his compensation was concerned.

He had no expertise, no training, and no experience in commercial real estate development. The businessman who had hired him became too busy to teach Merrill all he needed to know. There were questions that Merrill felt he should ask, but he didn't know where to go for the answers. Nevertheless, he considered himself fortunate. There would be plenty of time to learn the business once things settled down. He forgot how important it is to stay centered in reality when you're on the job.

About two years into this major venture, the price of crude oil declined sharply. Although Merrill was aware that the member of the family who owned his and other companies were major players in the Middle East oil business, he was oblivious to their dependency on high prices for crude oil to finance their various projects around the world. His boss reassured him that although a little belt tightening was required, it was nothing to worry about. What his boss didn't tell him was that the cash coming in to pay monthly expenses and short-term financing notes was rapidly drying up.

A business pro would have asked probing questions and recognized trouble on the horizon. But Merrill was a novice who dismissed stories in the media that cast doubt on the ability of his company to complete its massive project. He was still getting paid a substantial salary, and his perks continued, although his annual bonus was a fraction of what it had been in the two previous years. "Hey! Don't worry about it, big guy," Merrill thought to himself. "You never received any bonus when you were an educator." But then, he hadn't relied on wishful thinking as an educator, either.

The day Merrill was laid off, his boss held a brief meeting to announce that the family could no longer support the project. They would probably default on their loans. There were just too many projects to finance, and with the drop in the price of oil, something had to give. Merrill was out of a job for the first time in his adult life.

More than six years have passed since that awful August. Scholarships, student loans, and summer jobs helped Merrill's children pay their own way through college. Merrill has held a series of low-level jobs in business. None of them has lasted long enough to lead to an executive position. He has never considered re-entry to the world of education where he was once successful. When he got out, he swore never to return—a decision responsible for a loss of opportunity for Merrill and for education. Instead of dealing creatively with the normal boredom of a too-familiar job, he had run away. Thinking money could cure his dissatisfaction, he became a businessman and was brought down by his naïveté. Then he refused to reassess his situation and return to a career for which he was realistically suited.

Reflections on Chasing Windmills
Only Makes You Tired

Unlike Don Quixote, Merrill was not simpleminded. Nor was he an idealist. He could be charming, or he could be tough. Basically a self-disciplined, decent man, Merrill started out with clear-cut personal and career goals. Nothing distracted him from achieving what he set out to accomplish.

Yet he was vulnerable—even as Alonso Quixano had been—and off he went in his luxury sedan into a world he didn't understand. Both Don Quixote de la Mancha's and Merrill's sad stories show that getting involved in impractical schemes can lead to disillusionment. And both greed and naïveté can cost you dearly.

Lessons Learned from Chasing Windmills
Only Makes You Tired

Choosing your career or job can be a hit-or-miss affair. Trade-offs must be considered; we are not perfect people and we don't live in a perfect world. Some of us will choose the wrong careers or jobs. Others will be forced by circumstances to do work we don't like. We may even, like Merrill, trade in an appropriate career for an inappropriate one. Nevertheless, there are a few points worth considering in connection with making realistic job or career choices.

• Choose work that is sufficiently meaningful to you to inspire your best efforts. Without commitment to your work, you just get by.

• No matter how accomplished you are, be selective about the challenges and opportunities you accept.

• While you're growing up, it's usually best to put off deciding on your future job or career until you are a high-school senior or a college student.

• Minimize risks by choosing a job for which you have the training and temperament to succeed.

• Becoming an expert requires sacrificing pleasures and opportunities that distract you from your goal.

• All jobs get boring. But boredom doesn't necessarily indicate that it's time to move on to a new job. It may provide a chance to pursue interests outside work or to approach work more creatively. The key is to balance the satisfactions you find in your work with those in your personal life.

• Choose a job for the satisfaction it can bring you. Money and perks alone can't provide satisfaction unless the work interests you.

• If you choose the wrong job or career and want to leave it, analyze where you went wrong before choosing a new direction.

• When changing jobs or professions, don't be rash about rushing into something entirely new, unless you're financially and emotionally prepared to fail.

• Success in your first career doesn't ensure success in a second, and success in either one or the other is always earned.

• And finally, be wise and cautious about accepting any job. No job is exciting every day, and you can't be successful simply because an attractive opportunity comes along. Strive to choose work that suits your abilities.

17

Now There's Something
You Don't See Every Day!

Once upon a time, or so we are told, students obeyed teachers and school principals. They respected rules and authority. All across the land, students went to class, competed in interscholastic athletic events, participated in extracurricular activities and student government, helped out with chores at home, and held part-time jobs. Most of them completed their homework on time, and only a few cut classes. Unruly pupils actually responded to correction.

Now these students were not wimps. They became titans of industry, government leaders, inventors, scientists, athletes, and even artists. Others worked in factories, schools, garages, and banks, or on farms. Many went off to war. Some became criminals and drifters. Later generations have reaped the harvest they sowed.

Today a certain longing for traditional values is emerging. Peace and happiness have an enduring quality. By formulating your own values, you too can find personal balance in a tumultuous world.

Frank could have been a model for a Norman Rockwell painting. He was one of those blue-eyed, freckle-faced, blond, and robust boys who played with frogs and carried a slingshot in the back pocket of his jeans. Frank played baseball, teased his sisters, and fought with his brothers. In the winter, he ice-skated on the pond in the park. In the summer, he fished with his father and brothers. In the autumn, they hunted deer and pheasants, while his mother and sisters did things moms and sisters did back then. It wasn't that moms and sisters made a conscious decision to exclude dads and brothers from learning how to cook, shop, sew, wash and iron clothes, or how to make jams and jellies nor was there any conscious conspiracy on the part of the males to exclude females from their bonding experiences; it was the way things were during Frank's childhood.

Frank took his schooling seriously, but not too seriously. Although he wasn't a bully, he was involved in a playground skirmish or two, and he didn't always come out the winner (if there is ever a winner in such matters). Frank helped decorate the gym for school dances, was a member of the school wrestling team, and was on the yearbook staff in his senior year.

Following high-school graduation, Frank and several classmates went to the state university. During

his freshman year there, Frank and three of his hometown chums roomed together in a dormitory. There-
after, they lived in a small apartment near the campus.

None of these four farm boys had a scholarship.
They paid their expenses with savings accumulated
while working on the farm back home and with what
they earned in part-time jobs while in college.

Frank and his hometown buddies spent long nights
studying, were inspired by dedicated professors, and
dealt with prejudice against farm boys. They attended
football and basketball games. Their romances were
intense, but didn't last. One of their best friends was
killed in an automobile accident, another dropped out
of school because of a lack of funds, and still another
left school to earn a living for his new wife and the
child they accidentally conceived.

Frank was an excellent student. He studied in all
his courses, turned in his assignments on time, and
read extra resource materials. He visited his professors during their office hours to clarify concepts dis-
cussed in the classroom.

In his senior year, Frank, like most college students, thought about what he was going to do after he
graduated. He might join one of the large food-
packaging companies that was recruiting on campus.
They offered a respectable salary, a nice benefits plan,
an attractive retirement program, and the opportunity to develop new products for their rapidly growing
convenience food line. The U.S. Department of Agri-
culture also offered him a job. Along with security and
opportunity, it promised him his own laboratory for
research on the healthfulness of meat products. In ad-

dition, because he had made the Dean's List for four straight years and was graduating magna cum laude, Frank was offered several graduate school fellowships. To further complicate matters, Frank had fallen in love with Sally. She exuded self-confidence, she made him happy; she didn't expect him to become either rich or famous, but she wasn't going to put up with his achieving less than he could. Two weeks after graduation, Frank and Sally were married. This was no real surprise to anyone who knew either of them. What came as a shocker was their decision to buy Frank's parents' general store and move back to his hometown. His parents appreciated sweat equity, so they took back Frank and Sally's note for a friendly buyout. They knew Frank and Sally would make good on their promise to pay.

Frank and Sally aren't glamorous, as people who make big time buyouts in corporate America may be. Moreover, Frank turned down careers that ensured him the ability to provide quite comfortably for his family. He also turned down graduate schools. But what Frank and Sally wanted was to make it on their own in a familiar environment. Although the risks were greater, so was the potential reward.

Sally expanded the dry goods side of their general store. Frank specialized in butchering, and his reputation attracted customers from neighboring communities. They've had some close calls trying to pay bills on time. While their credit policy has been a real help to people in their town, their collection ratio has room for improvement.

Sally has given birth to three children, one of whom

is physically disabled. Frank has been on the town council for a number of years. Politics aren't as lively as in the big city, but every town needs governing, and Frank has been willing to do the job. Sally was twice elected to the school board. She was instrumental in helping the administration raise funds for two computers for each classroom. Sally and Frank still work hard at the general store. Most of their profits have gone back into the business. Their children work with them on weekends and after school.

Just in case you think their story is just too good to be true, be assured they've had the problems that parents have in other places. There has been worry about their children: failing grades, fighting at school, staying out too late, running with the wrong crowd, getting speeding tickets, breaking arms and hearts. They've even had a child arrested for smoking pot.

Neither Frank nor Sally has ever seen the Manhattan skyline or taken the Lexington Avenue Express from Grand Central Station to Wall Street. But there are folks in New York who have never caught a rainbow trout or walked across town at night without fear. And you can find good and happy people living in both places.

Reflections on Now There's Something You Don't See Every Day!

Frank had his ups and downs, but never stayed down for long. He had to decide whether or not to go to college, to attend class, to study or to party. He always did what he said he would do and never made less than his best effort. He complained a little, but did not lament his lot in life. When it was his turn to step up to the plate, he hit a home run. Sally is a capable teammate. They balance each other's hitting slumps, and they win more games than they lose.

Either Frank or Sally could have been successful in other jobs. They read serious books and love to attend plays, the ballet, and the symphony when they visit the city. They are both informed about world events, have a good handle on money management, and are very well invested for their future.

Rather ordinary? Yes! They are hardworking, honest people who exercise their right to vote. Both have made a difference in their community. They take pride in their family and work through their problems.

Perfect? No! But happy and ambitious enough to maintain that competitive edge necessary to overcome the just-getting-by syndrome. Now there's something you don't see every day!

Lessons Learned from Now There's Something You Don't See Every Day!

The lessons in Frank's story are straightforward and relevant to us all.

• You never achieve high marks in school or recognition for your work without making a draw from your sweat-equity account.

• Exceptionally good students have fun, but finish their homework first.

• A good education prepares you to make good choices.

• Making the right choices involves uncertainty and risk.

• The rewards you get are often different from the rewards you expect.

• You don't have to live in a big city to be well educated and culturally aware. If you lack an education or let your mind atrophy, you'll be disadvantaged wherever you are.

• If you think it's too tough to achieve success in a city, try making a difference in your hometown.

• Hard work and honest labor don't always pay huge dividends, but they don't give you a guilty conscience either.

• Laziness and deceit never pay any worthwhile return.

• If you make smart choices for yourself, you can be happy wherever you live and however you earn a living.

• You can't avoid problems: There is no running away, no place to hide. Whether rich or poor, you'll have to cope. How well you cope and adapt makes a big difference.

• You won't always have the wisdom, insight, and judgment to make the best choices. But after you have sought advice, you should make your own decisions. If you let other people make them for you, you surrender one of your most important freedoms.

• People change, times change, and societies change. The value of an educated mind, worthwhile work, and community service endure.

18

I Just Can't Wait Until . . .

Sigmund Freud is the father of psychoanalysis. He believed that people often work hard to reduce their anxieties and frustrations. Some attempts to reduce stress are healthy, some are not.

Most students worry about grades, which is normal when not carried to an extreme. Dropping out of school, however, is not a healthy way to reduce concern about grades. It is better to do the best you can in your studies and learn to enjoy school. Why then do so many students say they just can't wait until graduation? What is so important about school being over? Will there really be no pressures or demands to deal with then? Sure there will be. So learn to like handing in homework on time and preparing adequately for examinations. Be happy that your tests are over or that you've passed a course and another milestone has been reached. Participate in extracurricular activities. Make new friends. Have fun being a student. You'll meet frustrations and anxieties as an adult, so you'd better learn now how to enjoy yourself along the way.

Players say missing the pleasure of the moment can be seen in sports as well as in school. "Just wait until next year," "I'll sure be glad when this season is over," or "I can't wait until that loser isn't playing on our team." Whatever happened to enjoying the competition and the season?

At work you hear, "I can't wait until the new boss shows up," "I can't wait until the new owners take over," or "I'd give anything if I could retire today."

This was the day Mario had told his friends and colleagues that he'd looked forward to all during his career. This was Mario's last day at the office. He had reached the magic age of retirement.

Arriving at his office at the normal hour, Mario and his secretary of nine years packed all his personal belongings into cardboard boxes. At midmorning, he met with Annette, a young, bright, and capable executive. Beginning on the following Monday, Annette would be stepping up to assume the broader responsibilities of her former boss's position. During lunch, Mario bid final farewell to his staff. Admonishing them to support their new boss and challenging them to continue to excel under her guidance, he presented each one with a small gift, a token of his appreciation for their enduring loyalty and support.

Shortly before three o'clock, his wife and children met Mario in his office and walked with him to the company cafeteria where a nice reception had been arranged in his honor. More than two hundred people joined Mario and his family there. After everyone had enjoyed the splendid hors d'oeuvres, the division president began the formalities by introducing Mario's family. Then he reminisced about the high points of Mario's career. He was followed by several of Mario's co-workers, who spoke well of Mario and gave him gag gifts that were in stark contrast with the beautiful gold watch the company provided to all of its retirees with more than thirty years of service. Mario took the podium last. He began by thanking everyone for the help they'd been to him throughout his career and then, with moist eyes, he wished them well.

Colleagues crowded around Mario, shaking his hand, patting his back, or hugging and kissing him. Finally, Mario picked up his gifts and went back to his office. After one final look around what had been his home away from home for so many years, Mario carried the boxes to his car with his family's help.

As he drove home with his wife, Mario chatted about the people he'd miss and what he'd do next week, now that he was free. Mario also reflected on how he'd only recently reached the point in his career that he'd striven toward for so many years. Suddenly his happiness over retirement wasn't as great as he'd imagined it would be.

Reflections on
I Just Can't Wait Until . . .

Moving from one phase of life to another reduces current anxieties and introduces new ones.

Think about this for a moment. A student has difficulty getting along with one of her teachers and with four classmates. She thinks, "I wish school were over. I can't stand it. I just can't wait until next year." In the twinkling of an eye her wish is granted and she finds herself in the next school year. Not only has she not learned to resolve or understand interpersonal conflicts, she has also shut herself off from enjoying the good relationships of last year with other teachers and classmates. What if, as is likely to happen, she finds in the new school year that she can't get along with two of her teachers and five of her classmates? Will she wish this school year were over as well?

At work, if someone says, "I wish I had a new job," you may wonder: Why do you want a new job? Do you want an opportunity to start anew? To rid yourself of past obstacles? Or you need to change to an environment in which you can excel? What is limiting you in your present circumstance? If you had a new job would you work harder or smarter? Would you be happier?

Think about the wish to retire. You may not be physically able to play golf when you retire. You may not have the money to travel to new and exotic places. You won't necessarily have any more opportunity to enjoy your children or grandchildren than you did before you retired. So why should you want to wait until you're past your most productive years to begin enjoying life?

Lessons Learned from
I Just Can't Wait Until . . .

As a mortal with only a limited amount of time to achieve your goals, you ought to enjoy life as you go along. Happiness is too important to put off until tomorrow. Here are a few thoughts:

• Putting off doing your homework reduces the time you have to complete it and increases your anxiety over not having worked on it earlier.

• Your school years end but your education does not. So why be in a hurry to end your education at school?

• When you live solely for the future, you miss the possibilities in each day, and you may find your future to be very different from what you had imagined it would be.

• Time is a commodity equally allotted to all of us. Most of the other commodities we enjoy are a direct reflection of how wisely we use this everyday resource.

• When you procrastinate about doing important things, you become bitter over your failure to do them.

• Do the most important things on your to-do list first, the second most important things second, and so on. And because life is more than work, include personal as well as work-related items on your list.

177

• Things that can be done at any time never become important enough to do now.

• People who use their time wisely have more time to have fun than people who waste time.

• Not using your time wisely at work reduces your overall effectiveness, can result in having to work overtime, can force you to impose on others for help, and can result in a bad performance appraisal.

• Careful deliberation helps you act effectively. Prolonged deliberation gets in the way of your acting effectively.

• The only bad habits you never conquer are the ones you put off doing something about.

• The best remedy for having misused your time in the past is to use it more efficiently in the present.

• If you put off being happy until your retirement, you'll probably find little joy when you do retire, because all your life you'll have worked too long and too hard at developing a bad habit—putting off happiness.

• And finally, it is far better to live well than to spend your life getting ready to live well.

19

The Triumph of Personal Achievement

While there is pressure on all of us to excel, our greatest achievements will probably never be publicly recognized. Moreover, the sum total of our accomplishments is greater than any single achievement.

Personal success is never static. It usually comes in small steps leading to other small steps that lead to broader achievement. In school, students who earn high marks, perhaps straight A's, don't earn them on the day their teachers prepare report cards. High marks are earned through a laborious process that starts with just showing up in class. Then, paying attention is followed by taking notes, completing assignments, and studying for exams. Of course, some students are more gifted intellectually than others and can spend less time studying to excel. But all students must work to do their best. And an average student who has good teachers, helpful parents, and disciplined study habits can learn a lot and earn an A or two through concentrated effort.

The benchmarks of success vary from student to student. Thousands of students, unfortunately, don't live in nurturing homes. For them, going to school each day is a greater victory than it is for more fortunate students. So is getting a first B or actually graduating. Trying out for a school athletic team is as important a personal achievement for some as scoring the winning point is for others. Participation in the student government, in the band, in plays—each represents a step forward for someone.

All your life, there are challenges to meet, and defeats and disappointments to overcome. Personal achievement takes effort. You can't win it in a lottery or inherit it from a rich relative.

Accepting yourself is important. So is being accepted by others. What others think of you affects how you feel about yourself, and how you feel about yourself affects what you think of others. But you are ultimately in control of how you feel about yourself. And the better you feel about yourself, the more you're in control of your own destiny. The triumph of personal achievement is found in feeling good about yourself.

Isolation and rejection affect everyone. Whether they take the form of not having friends, not being accepted by teachers, receiving a bad performance review at work, being subjected to a scathing review by a critic—damage to your self-esteem hurts. That's why peer pressure works. That's why parents care about who their children's friends are. Fear of rejection can keep even mature people from asking someone for a date. Fear of failing to make the team keeps many young people from trying out.

Choosing to be isolated is difficult but it may be wise. For instance, if you must choose between the wrong friends and no friends, you need uncommon courage to make the best decision for yourself. And the right decision will be painful because you may be lonely until you're able to make the right kind of friends.

As you enter adulthood, making choices that lead to personal achievement becomes increasingly difficult. You can very often benefit from the advice of friends, teachers, and family. A wealth of good advice is also available in books and audiotapes. Moreover, giving good advice, as strange as it seems at first, may be the best thing a poor boss ever does for you.

After high school, the next step in personal achievement may be going to college or to a trade or technical school. Applying for your first job is a step toward personal achievement too. Showing up for work regularly is another. Doing your best at an honest job is always gratifying.

The path to personal achievement is rarely, if ever, clearly marked. You will encounter dragons, fiery pits, fallen trees, and many other obstacles along the way. Some of them will be real, some imagined. As hard as you try, you can never be fully prepared for them all. At times, you will be bitterly disappointed. At others, you will be discouraged. But the triumph of personal achievement is worth pursuing and is always defined in terms of your own abilities and temperament.

Personal achievement is a moving target. It is both exciting and exacting. It can't be measured by report cards or personal wealth. The triumph of personal achievement is, among other things, having the courage to overcome your weaknesses, the determination to bounce back from failure, the tenacity to persevere in difficult circumstances, the willingness to selflessly share your time and talents with other people, and the peace of mind—the easy conscience—that accompanies repeated small victories. So never give up on yourself!

Every man, woman, and child has the inalienable right to feel good about himself or herself, to have self-respect, to work through problems, and to overcome past failures. We all have the right to attain anything we are willing to earn. Personal achievement rarely brings immediate rewards and recognition. Doing your best at what you do every day may never lead to public acclaim, but it will lead to personal satisfaction.

There are no guarantees, no entitlements—and few real limits—placed on what you can achieve as you strive to live a good and rewarding life.